Facts about
KOREA

HOLLYM

Facts about Korea
Revised 1997 edition
Copyright © 1993
by Korean Overseas Information Service
All rights reserved

First published in 1997
by Hollym International Corp.
18 Donald Place, Elizabeth, New Jersey 07208 USA
Phone : (908) 353-1655   Fax : (908) 353-0255

Published simultaneously in Korea
by Hollym Corporation; Publishers
6th fl., Core Bldg., 13-13 Kwanchol-dong, Chongno-gu
Seoul 110-111, Korea
Phone : (02) 735-7554   Fax : (02) 730-5149

ISBN : 1-56591-051-6

Printed in Korea
by Sarmhwa Printing Co.

Foreword

Korea was ruled by a single government for almost 13 centuries, after Shilla absorbed its two neighbors, Koguryŏ and Paekche, into its administrative domain and unified the peninsula in the seventh century. As a result of the cold war power game following World War II, the nation was divided by a tightly guarded Military Demarcation Line, which still remains a international concern. The Korean War (1950-53) was a tragic experience for the entire Korean people, who have long been a homogeneous nation speaking one language and sharing the same traditions and culture.

The scar of the three-year internecine war was deep and painful but, ever optimistic and hard-working, Koreans have successfully recovered. During the past three decades, Koreans have achieved miraculous economic growth. They have, at the same time, made strenuous efforts to build a mature, democratic state guaranteeing public welfare by carefully incorporating modern Western ideologies into their own political concepts and traditions. Symbolizing the success of these efforts, the 1988 Seoul Olympic Games and the 1993 Taejŏn Expo demonstrated the dynamism of the nation's modern development and its rapid progress toward becoming an advanced industrial nation.

This small booklet is a humble attempt to offer information about Korea, its land, people, history, culture, economy, government, society, traditions and modern accomplishments, to all who wish to know about the country for whatever reasons. It is hoped that this compact overview will prove useful in whetting the ever-spreading desire to learn more about Korea and in building bonds of friendship around the world.

Contents

Land and People

Land

The Korean Peninsula extends southward from the north eastern section of the vast Asian continent, spanning 1,000 kilometers north to south. It shares most of its northern border with China and touches Russia. The northernmost point is Yup'ojin in Onsŏng-gun, Hamgyŏngbuk-do Province, and the southernmost point is Marado Island, Cheju-do Province. The westernmost point is Maando Island in Yongch'ŏn-gun, P'yŏng-anbuk-do Province, and the easternmost is Tokdo Islets in Ullŭng-gun, Kyŏngsangbuk-do Province. Since 1948, the peninsula has been divided into two parts, the Republic of Korea in the south and the Democratic People's Republic of Korea in the north.

The Korean Peninsula is 222,154 square kilometers, almost the same site as the U.K. or Romania. The administrative area of the Republic of Korea is 99,392 square kilometers, slightly larger than Hungary or Portugal and a little smaller than Iceland.

Korea has a varied terrain, though about 70 percent of the territory is mountainous. The spectacular T'aebaek mountains run the full length of the east coast, where the lashing tides of the East Sea, have carved out sheer cliffs and rocky islets. The western and southern slopes are very gentle, forming plains and many offshore islands honeycombed with inlets. The irregular shoreline is dotted with over 3,000 islands.

The peninsula has many scenic mountains and rivers, so Koreans often call it the "land decorated with golden embroidery." The highest peak is Mt. Paektusan, or the Ever White Mountain, which stands 2,744 meters high

on the northern borderline facing Manchuria. This extinct volcano, with a crater named Ch'ŏnji, or Heavenly Lake, on its top, is shrouded with a mythical aura as the site of the first kingdom in Korean history, dating back some 5,000 years. The mountain is also noted as a rich depository of wildlife.

Considering the size of its territory, Korea has a relatively large number of rivers and streams which have played important roles in developing industries and lifestyles. Both of the two longest rivers, the Amnokkang River (Yalu, 790km) and the Tuman-gang River (Tumen, 521km), originate at Mt. Paektusan and flow to the west and the east, respectively, to form the peninsula's northern border. In South Korea, the Naktong-gang River (525km) and the Han-gang River (514km) are the two major rivers responsible for irrigation and industrial water supply. The Han-gang River flows through Seoul, the capital of the Republic and serves as a lifeline for the large population in the central region, including Seoul's 11 million residents. The river also played a significant part in the development of Korea's ancient civilization.

The Yellow Sea, lying between Korea and the People's Republic of China, and the ocean south of the peninsula form a continental shelf with the shallow sea floor providing valuable resources for the fishing industry. Surrounding the peninsula on three sides, the sea has played a remarkable role in Korean life since ancient times, contributing to the early development of shipbuilding and navigation skills. In recent years, the seabed off the southwestern coast has been explored for petroleum deposits.

Climate

Korea enjoys four seasons and a variety of different weather types. Located in the East Asian monsoon belt, the peninsula has hot, humid summers and long, dry, cold winters. Spring and autumn are rather short, but very pleasant with crisp weather and many days of

sunshine.

Temperatures range from a low of −15°C (5°F) in winter to a high of 34.7°C (94.5°F) in summer. The three months of June, July, and August have the heaviest rains, with July usually being the wettest month of the year. Winter starts in late November and lasts until early March. It is dominated by a high pressure zone caused by cold blasts of air from Siberia. There is little precipitation and the skies are usually clear. Winter in South Korea is generally not as severe as it is in the North.

The weather in early spring is somewhat unpredictable with frequent rainfalls and gusty winds carrying yellow dust from northern China. But in mid-April, the country enjoys balmy weather with the mountains and fields garbed in brilliant wild flowers. Farmers prepare seedbeds for the annual rice crop at this time.

Autumn is beautiful with crisp air and blue skies. The countryside is colored in a variety of mellow hues. This is the time for harvest and consequently the time for thanksgiving. Autumn in Korea is a delightful season featuring many folk festivals rooted in ancient agrarian customs.

People and Population

The Koreans are one ethnic family speaking one language. Linguistic and anthropological studies as well as legendary sources clearly distinguish Koreans from the Chinese and the Japanese. Sharing distinct physical characteristics, they are believed to be descendants of several Mongol tribes which migrated onto the Korean Peninsula from Central Asia.

Koreans were a homogeneous people by the begin-

ning of the Christian era. In the seventh century A.D. they were politically unified for the first time by the Shilla Kingdom (57 B.C.-A.D. 935) and subsequently witnessed a great cultural flowering.

The Korean people struggled successfully for millennia to maintain their cultural and political identity despite the influence of neighboring China and the more recent aggressive inclinations of the Japanese. They are a proud people with one of the longest national histories in the world.

The Republic of Korea had a population of 45.2 million in 1996 and registered a density of 455 persons per square kilometer. The population of North Korea was 23.6 million in 1996.

Fast population growth was once a serious social problem in the Republic, as in most other developing nations. Owing to successful family planning campaigns and changing attitudes, however, population growth has been curbed remarkably in recent years. The annual growth rate was 0.88 percent in 1996.

A notable trend in the population structure is that it is getting increasingly older. The 1996 statistics showed that 40.9 percent of the total population was under 25. The number of people of productive age, 15 and above, rose from 24,751,000 in 1980 to 35,033,000 in 1996.

Another distinct but unwelcome phenomenon is the continuing migration of rural residents to cities, resulting in heavy population concentrations. Currently, one out of every four Koreans lives in Seoul. Specialists predict that the urban population will increase to 80.6 percent in 2000, up from 74.4 percent in 1990. To cope with the growing urban problems caused by such an imbalance, the Government has prepared a long-term manpower development plan. The plan aims at dispersing population to provincial areas through the relocation of economic activities and balanced land development.

Minority groups are almost nonexistent in Korea, apart from some 30,000 Chinese who are mostly long-term residents in the capital area.

Language

Koreans all speak and write the same language, which has been a crucial factor in their strong national identity. Modern Korean has several different dialects including the standard one used in Seoul and central areas, but they are similar enough that speakers do not have trouble understanding each other.

Linguistic and ethnological studies have established that the Korean language belongs to the Ural-Altaic language group of Central Asia, which also includes Turkish, Hungarian, Finnish, Mongolian, Tibetan and Japanese. Korean bears considerable resemblance to Japanese in grammatical structure.

The Korean alphabet, called *Han-gŭl*, was invented in the 15th century by a group of scholars under the

The Korean Alphabet

Vowels	ㅏ	ㅑ	ㅓ	ㅕ	ㅗ	ㅛ	ㅜ	ㅠ	ㅡ	ㅣ
	a	ya	ŏ	yŏ	o	yo	u	yu	ŭ	i

Consonants	ㄱ	ㄴ	ㄷ	ㄹ	ㅁ	ㅂ	ㅅ
	k, g	n	t, d	r, l	m	p, b	s, sh

	ㅇ	ㅈ	ㅊ	ㅋ	ㅌ	ㅍ	ㅎ
		ch, j	ch' k'	k'	t'	p'	h

안녕하세요 (How do you do?)

an nyŏng ha se yo

patronage of King Sejong the Great (r. 1418-50), the fourth monarch of the Chosŏn Dynasty (1392-1910). Before the invention of these simple phonetic symbols, Korean was written by means of Chinese characters, which depend on a totally different linguistic system. Learning Chinese literature was so time-consuming that only a handful of privileged aristocrats were able to master it.

The Korean alphabet, which is considered one of the most scientific writing systems in use in the world, consists of 10 vowels and 14 consonants, which can be combined to form numerous syllabic groupings. It is simple, but systematic and comprehensive at the same time. *Hangŭl* is easy to learn and print, which has greatly contributed to Korea's high literacy rate and advanced publication industry. It is also easily appliable to computer systems.

History

The history of human activity in Korea can be traced far into the Paleolithic period, about 500,000 years ago.

The beginning of Korean history is often dated to 2333 B.C. when King Tan-gun, a legendary figure born of the son of Heaven and a woman from a bear-totem tribe, established the first kingdom named Chosŏn, literally meaning the "Land of the Morning Calm." While the historicity of the Tan-gun myth is disputed among scholars, it is known that ancient Korea was characterized by clan communities which combined to form small city-states. They rose and fell so that by the first century B.C. three kingdoms, Koguryŏ (37 B.C.-A.D.668), Paekche (18 B.C.-A.D.660) and Shilla (57 B.C.-A.D.935), had emerged on the Korean Peninsula and part of what is now known as Manchuria.

Ever since Shilla unified the peninsula in 668, Korea has been ruled by a single government and has maintained its political independence and cultural and ethnic identity in spite of frequent foreign invasions. Both the Koryŏ (918-1392) and Chosŏn (1392-1910) Kingdoms consolidated their dynastic power and flourished culturally, while repelling intruders like the Khitans, Mongols, Manchus and Japanese. In the late 19th century, Korea became the focus of intense competition among imperialist nations, China, Russia and Japan. In 1910, Japan annexed Korea and instituted colonial rule, bringing the Yi Dynasty of Chosŏn to an end and with it, traditional Korea. National liberation occurred in 1945 but was soon followed by territorial division. The Republic of Korea in the south has a democratic government, while the Democratic People's Republic of Korea in the north is ruled by a Communist regime.

The Dawn of History

Of all the legends and myths concerning the origin of the Korean people, the oldest and most often cited is about Tan-gun. The legend says that Prince Hwanung, the son of Heaven's supreme deity, descended on Mt. T'aebaeksan along with 3,000 servants and built the "City of God." He was a good ruler who taught his people over 360 useful trades and arts, including agriculture, medicine, carpentry, weaving and fishing.

At that time there were a bear and a tiger who wished to become human. He told them that if they remained in a dark cave and ate only garlic and mugwort for one hundred days, they would become human. The bear survived the ordeal and became a beautiful woman, but the tiger failed due to a lack of perseverance. The bear-woman married Hwanung and bore a son, Tan-gun, who later established a kingdom named Chosŏn in P'yŏngyang in 2333 B.C.

Tan-gun is the mythical progenitor of the Korean people. Today Koreans celebrate October 3, the day Tan-gun is said to have founded his kingdom, as National Foundation Day.

Chosŏn, or Ko-Chosŏn (Ancient Chosŏn) as modern Koreans prefer to call it to distinguish it from the other kingdom of the same name founded in the 14th century, is said to have lasted until the second century B.C. About this time the emperor of China's Han Dynasty, regarding Chosŏn as a major threat on the eastern flank of his empire, decided to conquer it.

China set up four military colonies in the northern half of the Korean Peninsula and Manchuria, but could not control them. Only one of them, Nangnang (Lolang in Chinese), believed to have been situated in the region of present-day P'yŏngyang (some scholars question its location), survived until the early fourth century A.D. as a center for trade and direct cultural contact between Korea and China.

A hunting scene from a sixth century Koguryŏ Tomb.

The Three Kingdoms

Korea's earliest recorded history is characterized by clan communities which combined to form small city-states. The city-states gradually united into tribal leagues with increasingly complex political structures. This state of affairs prevailed throughout the peninsula and southern Manchuria until roughly the beginning of the Christian era.

Among various tribal leagues, Koguryŏ (37 B.C.-A.D. 668), along the middle course of the Amnokkang River (Yalu), was the first to mature into a kingdom. Its belligerent troops conquered neighboring tribes one after another. They finally drove the Chinese out of Nangnang in 313 A.D. and expanded their territory deep into Manchuria.

These developments in the north had repercussions in the politically and culturally less advanced southern part of the peninsula. A group of refugees from Koguryŏ founded a new kingdom named Paekche (18 B.C.-A.D. 660) south of the Han-gang River in the vicinity of present-day Seoul.

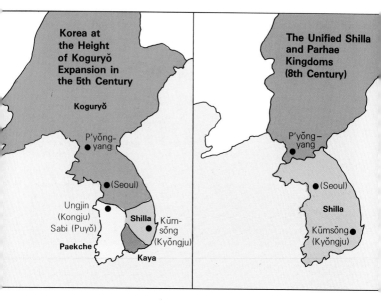

Korea at the Height of Koguryŏ Expansion in the 5th Century

Koguryŏ

P'yŏng-yang

(Seoul)

Ungjin (Kongju)
Sabi (Puyŏ)

Paekche

Shilla

Kŭm-sŏng
(Kyŏngju)

Kaya

The Unified Shilla and Parhae Kingdoms (8th Century)

P'yŏng-yang

(Seoul)

Shilla

Kŭmsŏng
(Kyŏngju)

The people of Paekche were evidently more peaceful than the ferocious warriors of Koguryŏ, so they kept moving south to avoid the threats of their northern rival. By the fourth century, they completely dominated the southwestern part of the peninsula. Paekche was firmly established as a prosperous and civilized state, trading extensively with China across the sea.

Shilla (57 B.C.-A.D. 935), which was geographically removed from Chinese influence, was at first the weakest and most underdeveloped of the three kingdoms. The last to adopt foreign creeds and ideas, its society was markedly class-oriented and developed remarkable power, drawing resources from its unique Hwarang (Flower of Youth) Corps and Buddhist teaching.

By the mid-sixth century, Shilla had brought under its control all of the neighboring Kaya Kingdoms, a group of fortified town-states that developed in the southeastern region from the mid-first century to the mid-sixth century. It effected a military alliance with T'ang China to subjugate both Koguryŏ and Paekche. But China was a

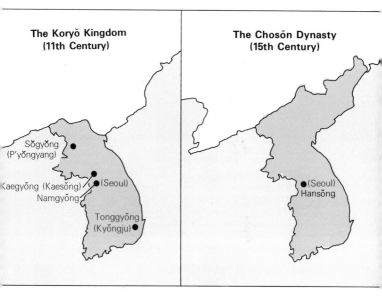

**The Koryŏ Kingdom
(11th Century)**

Sŏgyŏng
(P'yŏngyang)

Kaegyŏng (Kaesŏng)
Namgyŏng

(Seoul)

Tonggyŏng
(Kyŏngju)

**The Chosŏn Dynasty
(15th Century)**

(Seoul)
Hansŏng

dangerous ally. Shilla had to take up arms against China when the Chinese exposed their own ambition to incorporate the territories of Koguryŏ and Paekche into their own empire.

Although politically separate, the three kingdoms of Koguryŏ, Paekche and Shilla were related ethnically and linguistically. Each of them developed a sophisticated political structure and legal system and adopted Confucian ethics and Buddhist faith. Over the centuries, however, conflicts among them continued to grow with various and changing alliances between two against the other or against China or with China against the others.

Buddhism spread rapidly among the upper classes of these kingdoms after it was introduced in the fourth century through China. Rulers of all three kingdoms patronized Buddhism and used it to bolster their power. Korean monks traveled to China and India to study the scriptures and transmitted Buddhist literature and arts to Japan, playing a decisive role in the development of that country's ancient civilization.

Royal tombs in Kyŏngju, the former capital of the Shilla dynasty (57 B.C.-A.D. 935).

Unified Shilla and Parhae

Shilla's victory over China in 676 was a triumphant turning point in Korean history. Shilla succeeded in repelling the Chinese from the peninsula and achieved its first territorial unification. Following this, the people of Koguryŏ repulsed T'ang forces in Manchuria and the northern part of the peninsula, and established the Kingdom of Parhae in 698. This period has been referred to as that of the Northern and Southern Kingdoms.

For two and a half centuries, Shilla enjoyed peace and prosperity. Freed from the worries of domestic conflicts and external invasions, it achieved rapid development in the arts, religion, commerce, education and all other fields. The Shilla capital, present-day Kyŏngju, had a population of over one million. Its citizens led affluent lives and the city boasted magnificent royal palaces and Buddhist temples.

Buddhism flourished under the patronage of the nobility and court, exerting tremendous influence upon state affairs, artistic creation and ethics. Some of Korea's outstanding historical monuments are attributed to the creative genius and religious fervor of the artisans of this

A Buddhist pagoda dating back to the Paekche period (18 B.C.-A.D. 660).

time. Among the monuments representing the great cultural flowering of the period are Pulguksa Temple and Sŏkkuram Grotto Shrine, both located in the vicinity of Kyŏngju.

Shilla reached the peak of its prosperity and power in the mid-eighth century, but gradually declined thereafter. Conflicts among the nobility intensified, while rebel leaders claimed succession to the demolished dynasties of Koguryŏ and Paekche. In 935 the king of Shilla turned the reins of his state over to the court of the newly founded Koryŏ Kingdom.

In south central Manchuria, which had been part of Koguryŏ, Parhae was founded by a former Koguryŏ general, Tae Cho-yŏng. Parhae included not only people of Koguryŏ ethnic stock but also a large Malgal population.

Parhae established a five regional-capital system of government based on Koguryŏ's administrative structure and possessed an advanced culture also based on Koguryŏ to the extent that China named it "the flourishing land in the east".

At the height of its power, it occupied a vast territory

reaching to the Amur-gang River in the north and Káiyuan in Manchuria to the west. Early on, it came into conflict with T'ang and Shilla but later established peaceful relations with China. It also had diplomatic ties with the Turks and Japan.

Koryŏ

The founding monarch of Koryŏ (918-1392) was a general who had served under a rebel prince of Shilla. Choosing his native town, Song-ak, the present-day Kaesŏng, as the seat of his kingdom, he proclaimed a policy to recover the lost territory of Koguryŏ in Manchuria. Therefore he named his kingdom Koryŏ, from which the modern name Korea is derived. But over the five centuries of its existence, Koryŏ was never able to realize this ambition.

Koryŏ, however, did make outstanding accomplishments. Korean potters created a mysterious bluish-green glaze for celadon, making a monumental contribution to the world. The exquisitely inlaid Koryŏ celadon, representing the refined taste of the aristocrats of the time, was highly prized throughout East Asia including the Sung imperial court in China.

No less significant was the invention of the world's first movable metal type in 1234, which preceded Gutenberg by two centuries. About this time, Korean technicians also completed the herculean task of carving the entire Buddhist canon on large woodblocks. These woodblocks, numbering no less than 80,000, were intended to invoke the influence of Buddha for the repulsion of the Mongol invaders. Called *Tripitaka Koreana*, they are now stored at the historic Haeinsa Temple.

From the outset, the royal court of Koryŏ adopted Buddhism as the state religion. It flourished greatly, stimulating temple construction and the carving of Buddhist images as well as icon paintings. But it also played a part in the decline of the Koryŏ court, as monks wielded excessive power. During the kingdom's later years,

The *Tripitaka Koreana* woodblocks in the Haeinsa Temple archives.

it was severely shaken by conflicts between scholar-officials and warriors and between Confucianists and Buddhists. The Mongol incursions which began in 1231 left Koryŏ as a Mongol vassal state for nearly a century despite courageous resistance from the Koryŏ people for over 20 years.

In the 10th century, the Koryŏ court adopted the Chinese system of civil service examination for the recruitment of officials by academic merit. But whereas in China the civil service system was open to men of any social status, in Korea it was monopolized by the families of higher officials.

Chosŏn

The date Confucianism was introduced in Korea was around the beginning of the Christian era, almost at the same time as the earliest written Chinese material entered the peninsula. But neither Shilla nor Koryŏ recognized its intellectual and moral strengths. Confucianism became a powerful instrument for reorganizing the state and society and for infusing new discipline into intellectual life in the 14th century with the inception of the

Kŭnjŏngjŏn, the throne hall in Kyŏngbokkung Palace in Seoul, was originally built in 1392.

Chosŏn Dynasty (1392-1910), which is better known in the West as the Yi Dynasty.

The early rulers of Chosŏn replaced Buddhism with Confucianism in order to counter the dominant Buddhist influence and to appropriate the great wealth accumulated by monasteries during the Koryŏ period. Neo-Confucian theories of state and society provided the ideological basis for wide-reaching reforms in the hands of the elite of the new dynasty. Confucian ethics and values came to dominate social structure and behavior through the following centuries.

The Chosŏn rulers governed with a well-balanced, sophisticated political system. The civil service examination system was firmly established as the main avenue of recruitment for government office. The examinations formed the backbone of social mobility and intellectual activity during the period. The society in general highly valued academic learning while disdaining commerce and manufacturing.

During the reign of King Sejong (r. 1418-50), Chosŏn's fourth monarch, Korea enjoyed an unprecedent-

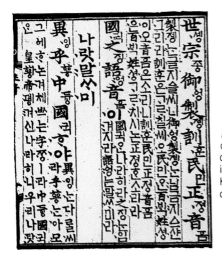

Han-gŭl, the Korean alphabet, originally called *Hunmin chŏng-ŭm* or "the correct sounds for the instruction of the people" was King Sejong's (r. 1418-1450) crowning achievement.

ed flowering of culture and the arts. Under his patronage, scholars at the royal academy invented the Korean alphabet, *Han-gŭl*, a highly scientific yet simple and effective system of writing. Sejong's rule marked a "golden age" in Korean history. It produced numerous inventions and progressive ideas in the areas of government administration, economy, the natural sciences, the humanities, music and medicine.

In the late 16th century, however, Korea experienced the trauma of a seven-year war with Japan. After the court of Chosŏn rejected a request by the Japanese warlord Toyotomi Hideyoshi to make way for his invasion of China, Hideyoshi launched a Korean campaign. Most of the peninsula was devastated, and numerous Korean artisans and technicians were forcibly taken to Japan.

At sea, Admiral Yi Sun-shin conducted a series of brilliant operations against the numerically superior Japanese naval forces. On land, voluntary peasant fighters and contingents of Buddhist monks gallantly engaged the enemy. The Japanese began to withdraw with the death of Hideyoshi and the war ended at last in 1598, having left a disastrous impact upon both Korea and Ming China.

From the early 17th century, a movement advocating practical studies gained considerable momentum among liberal-minded scholar-officials as a way to build a modern nation state. They strongly recommended agricultural and industrial improvements, and sweeping reforms in land distribution. The government of conservative aristocrats, however, was not ready to accommodate their ideas.

In the later half of the Chosŏn Dynasty, the government administration and the upper classes came to be marked by recurring factionalism. King Yŏngjo (r. 1724-1776) thus adopted a policy of impartiality to combat this and succeeded in strengthening the royal authority and securing political stability. He also instituted the Equalized Tax Law to ease the tax burden on the general populace and to address the compulsory military service problem, and initiated public works projects as well. His successor, King Chŏngjo (r. 1776-1800) maintained the policy of impartiality, established a Royal Library to store royal writings and records, and initiated other political and cultural reforms.

This period also witnessed the rise of *sirhak* or the school of practical learning among liberal-minded scholar-officials. A number of outstanding scholars wrote progressive writings recommending agricultural and industrial improvements, and sweeping reforms in land distribution. Unfortunately, most of their ideas were ignored, and the government stuck to its orthodox ways.

Korea remained a "hermit kingdom" adamantly opposed to the Western demands for diplomatic and trade relations in the 19th century. Korea adhered to its alliance with China, which was fighting for its own life against Western encroachment and could not help Korea. Japan, which had risen as a new industrial power, eventually stepped into the power vacuum and annexed Korea. The Chosŏn Dynasty ended in 1910.

Painting depicting the Independence Movement of March 1, 1919.

The Japanese Occupation and Korea's Independence Movement

Japan's government-general in Seoul was mainly interested in the economic exploitation of Korea. Japanese farmers and fishermen were encouraged to emigrate to Korea and were given land free or at low cost. Large quantities of rice were exported to Japan, while Koreans faced a serious food shortage. As the Japanese prospered on Korean resources, the Korean standard of life deteriorated drastically. As a result, hundreds of thousands of Korean farmers abandoned their farms and moved to Manchuria or Japan, only to find life no easier there.

Colonial rule stimulated the growth of nationalism among Koreans. Korean intellectuals were infuriated by Japan's official assimilation policy. They asserted their differences and struggled to distance themselves culturally from their colonial masters. In 1919, Koreans staged nationwide protests at the cost of thousands of lives. This independence movement failed to depose the Japanese, but gave Koreans strong bonds of national identity and patriotism, and led to the establishment of the Provisional Government in Shanghai and to an organized armed struggle against the Japanese colonialists in Manchuria.

The Founding of the Republic

Koreans welcomed the defeat of Japan in World War II with great joy and relief. However, their joy was short-lived. Liberation did not bring the independence for which the Koreans had fought so hard, but the inception of ideological conflict in a partitioned country.

The efforts of the Koreans to establish an independent government were frustrated by the U.S. in the South and the occupation of the North by the Soviet Union.

In November 1947, the United Nations General Assembly adopted a resolution which called for a general election under the supervision of a U.N. Commission. However, the Soviet Union refused to comply with the U.N. resolution and denied the U.N. Commission access to the northern part of Korea. The U.N. General Assembly adopted a new resolution calling for elections in areas accessible to the U.N. Commission.

The first elections in Korea took place on May 10, 1948, in the area south of the 38th parallel, and the Government of the Republic of Korea was inaugurated on August 15. A Communist regime was set up in the North under Kim Il-sung, a Stalinist ruler with absolute power.

On June 25, 1950, North Korea launched an unprovoked full-scale invasion of the South and started a war that lasted three years. As the Communist North Koreans campaigned to unify the country by force, the entire land was devastated and millions of people were left homeless and separated from their families. A cease-fire was signed in July 1953, and both sides have since gone through enormous changes in their efforts at rehabilitation.

Reunification remains the long-cherished but elusive goal of all Koreans on both sides of the vigilantly guarded Military Demarcation Line. The fall of Communism in the Soviet Union and Eastern Europe and the unification of Germany raised expectations in Korea that unification could be achieved in the not very distant future.

Some progress in promoting trust and cooperation between the two halves of the Peninsula was made in recent years. However, the threat of North Korea's suspected nuclear weapons development program has stood in the way of real forward movement, and there is still a long and bumpy road ahead before the proposed Korean Peninsula Energy Development Organization (KEDO) project for the construction of lightwater nuclear reactors gets under way in the North and other North Korean nuclear issues are completely settled.

Constitution and Government

The Constitution

The Republic of Korea has a democratic form of government based upon the separation of powers and a system of checks and balances. Sovereignty resides in the people, from whom all state authority is derived. The people's basic rights to freedom and to the benefits of and participation in government are guaranteed by the Constitution. In order to protect freedoms and rights to the maximum extent, the Constitution also provides for the independence of the three branches of the government: the executive, the legislature and the judiciary.

The Constitution of the Republic prescribes a presidential system for the executive branch of the government, designed to achieve strong and stable leadership based on a popular mandate. Personal liberty is fully guaranteed for all citizens, as are the freedoms of speech, the press, assembly and association. The Constitution promotes an atmosphere of national unity and harmony and sets the goal of the reunification of South and North Korea. It also respects international obligations, treaties, and the generally recognized rules of international law. The Constitution calls for free competition in presidential elections and limits presidential tenure to a single five-year term.

The Constitution guarantees the right to equality before the law regardless of sex, religion, or social status; freedom from arbitrary arrest; and freedom of residence. It also recognizes economic rights including the right to own property, the right and the duty to work, freedom of choice of occupation, and the right to collective bargaining. Explicitly emphasized, too, are the right to seek

The ROK's National Flag.

The *Mugunghwa,* or rose of Sharon, is the ROK's national flower.

The Korean National Flag, the *T'aegŭkki,* takes its name from the *t'aegŭk* circle in the center of the flag, is divided equally and is in perfect balance. The red upper section represents *yang* and the blue lower section *yin,* an ancient symbol of the universe—of the great cosmic forces that oppose each other but achieve perfect harmony and balance: fire and water, day and night, dark and light, construction and destruction, masculine and feminine, active and passive, heat and cold, plus and minus, and so on. The three bars at each corner also carry the ideas of opposition and balance. The three unbroken lines stand for heaven; the opposite three broken lines represent earth. At the lower left hand corner are two lines with a broken line between, symbolizing fire. Diagonally opposite is the symbol of water. The white background symbolizes the purity of the Korean people and their peace-loving spirit. The flag as a whole symbolizes the ideal of the Korean people developing forever in harmony with the universe.

happiness, optimum wages, fair compensation, and privacy.

The Constitution of the Republic was first adopted by the National Assembly on July 12, 1948, and promulgated on July 17. In the National Assembly's first session on May 31, 1948, which followed the U.N.-supervised general election of May 10, Taehan Minguk (the Republic of Korea) was chosen as the nation's

The National Anthem

Andante maetoso (Refrain)

Music: Ahn Eak-tae

Dong Hae Mul Gwa Paek Tu San I Ma Rŭ Go Dal T'o Rok

Ha Nŭ Nim I Bo U — Ha Sa U Ri Na Ra Man Se

(Refrain)

Mu — Gung Hwa Sam — Ch'ŏl Li HwaryŏGang — San

Dae Han Sa Ram Dae Han — Ŭ Ro Ki Ri Bo Chŏn Ha Se.

1. Until the East Sea's waves are dry, (and) Mt.Paektusan worn away,
   God watch o'er our land forever! Our Korea manse!
   Refrain:
   Rose of Sharon, thousand miles of range and river land!
   Guarded by her people, ever may Korea stand!

2. Like that Mt. Namsan armored pine, standing on duty still,
   wind or frost, unchanging ever, be our resolute will.

3. In autumn's, arching evening sky, crystal, and cloudless blue,
   Be the radiant moon our spirit, steadfast, single; and true.

4. With such a will, (and) such a spirit, loyalty, heart and hand,
   Let us love, come grief, come gladness, this, our beloved land!

official name. The Constitution was then drafted, adopted and promulgated. The President was elected and a government formed based on the principle of liberal democracy, and on August 15 of the same year, the nation was proclaimed to the world.

Since that time, the Constitution and the successive governments have undergone severe tests.

A National Assembly session.

The Legislature

Legislative power is vested in the National Assembly, a unicameral body. Two-thirds of the members of the National Assembly are elected by popular vote for a term of four years and the remaining seats are distributed proportionately among parties winning five seats or more in the direct election. This proportional representation system is aimed at encouraging legislative participation by leading technocrats through the political parties. The total number of Assembly members provided by the Constitution is no less than 200, with the exact number determined by statute. The parliamentary right to inspect government operations is recognized in the Constitution, as is the right to pass a recommendation for the removal of the Prime Minister or a State Council member from office. The National Assembly may also review the qualifications of its members and may take disciplinary actions against its members.

Major functions of the National Assembly include the power to propose, deliberate and approve or reject legislative bills, to finalize and inspect closing accounts of the national budget, to consent to the conclusion and ratification of treaties and to concur in the declaration of war or the conclusion of peace. The National Assembly is given the right to impeach the President and to approve his emergency orders, thereby enabling it to more effectively check any possible abuse of presidential prerogatives.

The National Assembly elects one speaker and two vice-speakers. An Assemblymember is not held responsible outside the Assembly for any opinions expressed or votes cast within the legislative chamber.

The Executive Branch

Standing at the apex of the executive branch of government, the President functions not only as head of state in domestic affairs but also represents the state in foreign relations. He has the express constitutional duty to safeguard the nation's independence and work for the peaceful reunification of the country. He is chairman of the State Council (cabinet) and has the power to appoint and dismiss the Prime Minister and cabinet ministers as well as other senior officials including heads of government agencies and offices, ambassadors. He serves as commander-in-chief of the armed forces and is empowered to grant amnesty, commutation and restoration of civil rights as prescribed by law. The President is elected through direct popular vote to serve a five-year term. He cannot be re-elected.

The President performs his executive functions through the State Council which is made up of 15 to 30 members and is presided over by the President, who is solely responsible for deciding all important government policies. The present State Council consists of the President (chairman), Prime Minister (vice chairman), two

Organization of the Government of the Republic of Korea

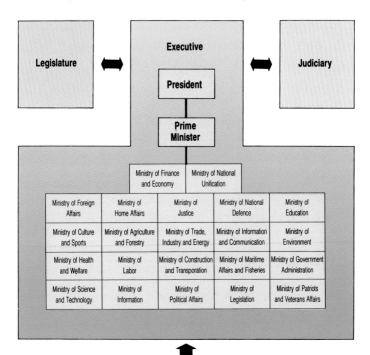

Legislature ⬌ **Executive**

President

Prime Minister

Ministry of Finance and Economy		Ministry of National Unification		
Ministry of Foreign Affairs	Ministry of Home Affairs	Ministry of Justice	Ministry of National Defence	Ministry of Education
Ministry of Culture and Sports	Ministry of Agriculture and Forestry	Ministry of Trade, Industry and Energy	Ministry of Information and Communication	Ministry of Environment
Ministry of Health and Welfare	Ministry of Labor	Ministry of Construction and Transporation	Ministry of Maritime Affairs and Fisheries	Ministry of Government Administration
Ministry of Science and Technology	Ministry of Information	Ministry of Political Affairs	Ministry of Legislation	Ministry of Patriots and Veterans Affairs

⬌ **Judiciary**

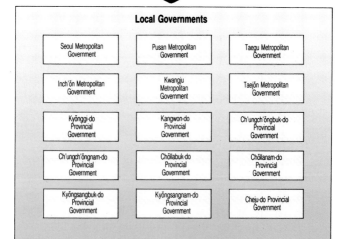

Local Governments

Seoul Metropolitan Government	Pusan Metropolitan Government	Taegu Metropolitan Government
Inch'ŏn Metropolitan Government	Kwangju Metropolitan Government	Taejŏn Metropolitan Government
Kyŏnggi-do Provincial Government	Kangwon-do Provincial Government	Ch'ungch'ŏngbuk-do Provincial Government
Ch'ungch'ŏngnam-do Provincial Government	Chŏllabuk-do Provincial Government	Chŏllanam-do Provincial Government
Kyŏngsangbuk-do Provincial Government	Kyŏngsangnam-do Provincial Government	Cheju-do Provincial Government

deputy prime ministers who are concurrently the Ministers of Finance and Economy and of National Unification, 16 heads of executive ministries, and two ministers of state. The Prime Minister is appointed by the President with the approval of the National Assembly. As the principal executive assistant to the President, the Prime Minister supervises the executive ministers under the direction of the President.

There are several organizations to aid the President and the State Council. These include the National Security Council which is chaired by the President and whose regular members include the Prime Minister, deputy prime ministers and concerned executive ministers, the Advisory Council on Democratic and Peaceful Unification and the National Economic Advisory Council. The Board of Audit and Inspection, under the direct jurisdiction of the President, is responsible for auditing the accounts of central and local government agencies, government corporations and related organizations. The Agency for National Security Planning is authorized to collect strategic intelligence to plan and coordinate the intelligence and security activities of the government.

The Republic of Korea is administratively divided into six metropolitan cities and nine provinces (*do*). The provinces are further divided into cities (*shi*), counties (*kun*), towns (*ŭp*) and townships (*myŏn*).

The Judiciary

The highest tribunal in the country, the Supreme Court examines and passes final decisions on appeals of the decisions of appellate courts in civil and criminal cases. Its decisions are final and indisputable, forming judicial precedents. The Chief Justice is appointed by the President to a single six-year term with the consent of the National Assembly, and the justices of the Supreme Court are appointed by the President on the recommendation of the Chief Justice. Judges at all lower courts are appointed by the Chief Justice with the consent of the

Conference of Supreme Court Justices.

There are five appellate courts which hear appeals of verdicts by district courts in civil and criminal cases. They hold their own trials and pass decisions for or against lower court verdicts. They may also pass decisions on administrative litigation filed by individuals or organizations against government decisions, orders or actions. District courts are established in major cities and exercise jurisdiction over all civil and criminal cases filed in the first instance. The Family Court hears matrimonial problems and cases involving juveniles. Its sessions are closed to the public in order to protect the privacy of individuals.

Political Parties

Numerous political parties sprang up after liberation in 1945 amid a national concern for creating democratic politics. A major political party, the Chayu-dang, or Liberal Party, was formed as the opposition took the form of the Minju-dang, the Democratic Party, in 1951. Party politics in the Republic experienced numerous twists and turns over the years.

Following the military coup in 1961, the ruling camp formed a new party, the Minjukonghwa-dang, the Democratic Republic Party, or DRP. Opposition parties banded together and established the Shinmin-dang, the New Democratic Party, or NDP, after a number of false starts.

After the assassination of President Park Chung Hee in 1979, a group of army officers forcefully created the 5th Republic. The Minjuchŏngui-dang, the Democratic Justice Party, or DJP, was led by President Chun Doo Hwan. The DJP gained a majority of seats at the National Assembly in the 1981 election. A political ban on activist politicians imposed in 1980 was lifted in 1985. Many of these activists formed the Shinhanminju-dang, the New Korea Democratic Party, or NKDP, and arose as the major challenge to the ruling party.

Street posters of candidates running in Korea's first local elections since 1960.

Massive, popular rallies in June 1987, resulted in political reform. A constitutional revision was worked out to allow direct election of the president, and Roh Tae-Woo was elected as President with 36.6 percent of the popular vote in December 1987. The ruling party, however, failed to capture a majority in the Assembly.

As the result, the opposition was able to apply pressure on political issues and against the ruling party as well. P'yŏnghwaminju-dang, the major opposition forces consisted of the Party for Peace and Democracy, or PPD, headed by Kim Dae-jung; the T'ongilminju-dang, Reunification Democratic Party, or RDP, organized by Kim Young Sam; and former Premier Kim Jong-pil's Shinminjukonghwa-dang, New Democratic Republican Party, or NDRP, based on Park's defunct DRP.

In 1990, the ruling DJP and the opposition RDP and NDRP worked out a compromise and merged to form a new party called the Minjuchayu-dang, the Democratic Liberal Party, or DLP. As of June 1996 the ruling party, the New Korea Party (the former DLP) has 151 of the 299 Assembly seats, while the major opposition party, the National Congress for New Politics has 79 seats, the United Liberal Democrats (the former NDRP) has 49 seats and minor parties share 20.

Kim Young Sam taking the presidential oath of office on February 25, 1993.

Presidents

President Kim Young Sam took the oath of office February 25, 1993, initiating the nation's first genuine civilian administration in 32 years. President Kim pledged to build what he called a "New Korea" through reform and change. He gained 42 percent of the popular vote, while his rival Kim Dae-jung garnered 34 percent.

In his inaugural speech, the President stated that the prerequisites to building a "New Korea" included eradicating corruption in officialdom and other parts of Korean society, reinvigorating the national economy and restoring national discipline. Before Kim Young Sam, there have been six presidents since the founding of the Republic of Korea in 1948 Syngman Rhee (Yi Sŭng-man) from 1948 to 1960; Yun Po-sun from August 1960 to May 1961; Park Chung Hee from 1963 to October 1979; Choi Kyu-hah from October 1979 to August 1980; Chun Doo Hwan from August 1980 to February 1988; and Roh Tae Woo from February 1988 to February 25, 1993.

Intra-Korean Relations

Territorial Division and the Korean War

At the close of World War II, Koreans looked forward to independence. However, their surging hopes and joy soon changed to despair and frustration. The Korean Peninsula, which had been under a single rule since the seventh century, was tragically divided into two as a result of postwar rivalry among the big powers.

In accordance with a secret decision at Yalta, the Soviet Union was permitted to disarm Japanese troops in the northern half of the Korean Peninsula as a reward for entering the war against Japan. This led to the Russians swooping rapidly into northern Korea at the close of the war. The United States proposed the 38th parallel as the division line. The US-USSR Joint Commission met in Seoul, but failed to reach an agreement for Korean independence.

The Korean question came before the United Nations General Assembly in 1947, resulting in a resolution that general elections would be held immediately to ensure independence and unification. The Soviet Union strongly objected to the U.N. decision and refused to allow U.N. delegates to enter the north. An election was held in southern Korea under U.N. supervision and the Republic of Korea, with a democratic presidential system, was officially formed in 1948. In the northern half of the peninsula, a communist regime was established under Russian influence.

On June 25, 1950, the North Koreans, led by Kim Il-sung and supported by the Soviet Union, launched an unprovoked invasion of the South. The South Korean troops fought bravely but proved no match for the heav-

Korean soldiers
recapturing Seoul
in September, 1950.

ily armed communists. Seoul fell in three days, and
almost all of Korea, except a corner in the southeast
known as the "Pusan perimeter," was overrun in about
a month. The U.N. General Assembly immediately decided to send troops to aid the South. Under the command
of General Douglas MacArthur, they soon began to
reverse the trend of the war. With some units reaching
the northern border of the Amnokkang River, unification seemed at last to be realized. But the Chinese in-
tervened, and the U.N. forces were compelled to retreat.
Fierce fighting continued until a cease-fire agreement was
finally reached on July 27, 1953.

The war bred mistrust, antagonism and hatred between
people on both sides. The protracted division since has
escalated ideological and cultural differences and led to
a diminishing sense of community. Millions of people
were separated from their families by territorial parti-
tioning and the war, and still there is no way for them
to hear from their relatives on the other side of the
Demilitarized Zone.

People with signs seeking to locate relatives long separated by the Korean War through a special long-run TV program aired in 1983 to help reunite dispersed families.

The Quest for Peaceful Unification

The Republic of Korea believes that unification must be achieved in a way that embodies the free will of the 70 million Korean people and that is totally free of violence. Its unification policy, therefore, is intended to promote the ideals of independence, democracy and peace, in contrast to North Korean schemes for unifying the peninsula by force under communism.

The Republic's unification policy is thus designed to peacefully and progressively eliminate the impediments to unification with the ultimate goal of integrating both societies into a single nation-state. It calls for steps to ease tension and military confrontation, to open both societies to each other, to initiate and expand exchanges and cooperation, and to consult about writing a constitution for a unified Korea leading to general elections to establish a single government.

On the basis of a mutual recognition of each other's socio-political system and on the principle of reciprocity,

South Korea since the early 1970s has continuously sought dialogue with the North. Seoul initiated South-North Red Cross talks on the reunion of separated families in 1971. On July 4, 1972, a South-North Joint Communiqué was issued calling for an end to mutual slander, the promotion of exchanges and the creation of a South-North Coordinating Committee to implement the terms of the declaration.

The seemingly auspicious initial steps toward reconciliation, however, failed to lead to any substantial result due to P'yŏngyang's insincere attitude. Furthermore, the North Koreans used the faltering dialogue to disguise their aggressive schemes. With the inauguration of the Fifth Republic in 1981, the Seoul Government stepped up its efforts for peaceful unification. Its repeated appeals for dialogue and exchanges, including President Chun Doo Hwan's request to hold a South-North summit conference, continued to fall on deaf ears until September 1984, when the South Korean Red Cross accepted a proposal by its North Korean counterpart to send relief goods for flood victims in the South. This accommodative gesture by the South temporarily broke the ice, resulting in the reopening of the Red Cross talks after a 12-year suspension and the initiation of trade and economic talks.

With official approval and under Red Cross auspices, sizeable numbers of private citizens separated from relatives on the other side crossed the Demilitarized Zone in both directions from September 20 to 23, 1985 for the first time since the end of the Korean War (1950-53). This was followed by preparatory sessions for a South-North parliamentary conference at the truce village of P'anmunjŏm and the South-North sports talks in Lausanne, Switzerland, on a possible North Korean role in the 1988 Summer Olympics hosted by Seoul.

Nonetheless, all of these channels of dialogue, except the Olympic talks, suddenly deadlocked once again when North Korea unilaterally canceled scheduled meetings in early 1986, claiming that the regular Korea-U.S. joint military exercises were incompatible with peaceful dialogue. This stance is considered an implausible pretext because the exercises had been conducted on an annual basis since 1976, and South-North talks have been held in the past while the exercises were under way. Moreover, North Korea has repeatedly been invited to send observers to verify their defensive nature. The historic South-North Prime Ministers talks were no exceptions, either. The South has made concessions to realize the South-North Prime Ministers talks at the earliest possible date. To this end, the South has accommodated many of North Korea's assertions concerning the agenda of the high-level talks and has done its utmost to open a path toward improved South-North Korean relations. Eight preliminary meetings were held before the first round of South-North High-Level talks on September 4, 1990 in Seoul.

Since then, high-level intra-Korean talks have been held eight times, the sites alternating between Seoul and P'yŏngyang. Both delegations were headed by prime ministers, who each met with the respective presidents of South and North Korea. The talks between the South and the North have been relatively fruitful.

At the Sixth Prime Ministers' talks in P'yŏngyang on February 19, 1992, the two prime ministers, Chung Won-shik of the South and Yon Hyong-muk of the North, exchanged letters on a Basic Agreement composed of a preamble and 25 articles.

The three historic accords were the Agreement on Reconciliation, Nonaggression and Exchanges and Cooperation, the Joint Declaration on the Denuclearization of the Korean Peninsula and the Agreement on the Formation of Subcommittees of South-North High-Level Talks.

With their effectuation, both sides agreed to form political, military and exchanges subcommittees to begin discussing concrete measures to implement the intra-

The Prime Ministers of South and North Korea exchanging an intra-Korean agreement on September 17, 1992.

Korean reconciliation accord.

The two Koreas inaugurated a joint nuclear control commission to discuss procedures and methods of mutual inspection of suspected nuclear weapons sites under the joint declaration. The Basic Agreement also prohibited the two Koreas from using force against each other or undertaking armed aggression against each other.

The eighth round of Prime Ministers' talks in P'yŏng-yang on September 17, 1992 further brought into effect the three affiliated accords in Reconciliation, Nonaggression, and Exchanges and Cooperation.

This progress in intra-Korean talks was considered the first step toward unification after 47 years of confrontation and enmity.

Due to suspicions about North Korea's nuclear arms development, however, intra-Korean relations once again became strained. The Joint Declaration bans the South and the North from testing, manufacturing, producing, receiving, possessing, storing, deploying or using nuclear weapons, and both parties agreed to bilateral, mutual nuclear inspections. But P'yŏngyang insisted that inspections by the International Atomic Energy Agency (IAEA) satisfied their obligations, while insisting that the U.S. military bases in the South needed to be inspected. The North threatened to discontinue all intra-Korean talks, including the Prime Minister's talks, if the Team Spirit exercise was resumed at the end of 1992.

Further, North Korea refused IAEA inspections and declared its intent to withdraw from the Nuclear Non-Proliferation Treaty (NPT) on March 12, 1993, raising the nuclear issue to the international level and bringing about tension in Northeast Asia and the rest of the world community.

After the U.N. Security Council adopted a resolution calling on North Korea to resolve the nuclear question, it came back to the negotiation table with the U.S. in mid-1993, and agreed to temporarily suspend its withdrawal from the NPT.

Finally, after a year and a half of U.S.-N.K. negotiations, the U.S. and the R.O.K. succeeded in persuading North Korea to sign an "Agreed Framework" on the nuclear issue in Geneva on October 22, 1994. In this, North Korea pledged to remain within the NPT, accept special and other inspections of its nuclear facilities by the IAEA, and freeze its nuclear activities now and in the future. P'yŏngyang also agreed to eventually dismantle its existing nuclear facilities, implement the Joint Declaration on Denuclearization, and resume South-North dialogue.

The Agreed Framework is viewed as a significant step toward resolving the North Korean nuclear issue once and for all. It also provided a basis for maintaining security and establishing a durable peace on the Korean Peninsula by easing tensions. The Framework is also taken as a key measure conducive to creating a favorable climate for South-North cooperation and opening the North's doors to the outside world. Furthermore, by as-

In June 1995, South Korea pledged to donate 150,000 tons of rice at no cost to help North Korea overcome its food shortage.

suming the central role in providing North Korea with light-water nuclear reactors agreed upon in the accord and more explicitly defined in a U.S.-DPRK Joint Statement of June 13, 1995, following five rounds of talks in Berlin and Kuala Lumpur, South Korea is hoping to help promote North Korea's development and thereby encourage North Korea to improve South-North relations.

However, the accord marks just the beginning of moves needed to resolve the nuclear issue altogether. Only when North Korea faithfully and thoroughly implements all of the provisions of the accord can the suspicions of N.K. nuclear weapons be completely dispelled, thus finally resolving the issue. Moreover, convinced that direct South-North talks are the only realistic way to improve intra-Korean relations, the ROK Government is urging North Korea to resume Seoul-P'yŏngyang dialogue as soon as possible.

Unification Policy of South Korea

Keynotes of the Korean National Community Unification Formula

The unification policy of the Kim Young Sam administration was outlined in his inaugural address of February 25, 1993, in which he emphasized, "... what is needed is not emotionalism but a reasoned national consensus on achieving this crucial goal." He thus established "a national consensus" as the priority task in preparing for unification.

Central to this policy is helping the North to actively participate in the international community as a full-fledged member, rather than remaining in isolation, and to induce it to change and reform itself. The North should break out of its inertia and rigid Cold-War thought patterns and behavior and come to the forum of reconciliation and cooperation, so that together, the two halves of the peninsula can strive for coexistence and unification while enjoying mutual prosperity.

South-North relations are bound to enter into a new phase following the death of Kim Il-sung, ruler of North Korea for nearly five decades. Having run into the limitations of its socialist system that has led to increasing international isolation and mounting economic woes, North Korea will almost certainly have to pursue an open-door policy and domestic reform in order to stabilize its post-Kim power structure.

The new global trends and anticipated changes in intra-Korean relations are urgently dictating that the nation pool its determination and energies to build a unified, democratic and prosperous homeland before the present century is out. Keeping a close watch on the shifting environment of the Korean Peninsula, President Kim more clearly defined the Republic's unification policy as well as its policy toward North Korea in a nationally-televised speech on the 49th Liberation Day on August 15, 1994.

Process of Unification

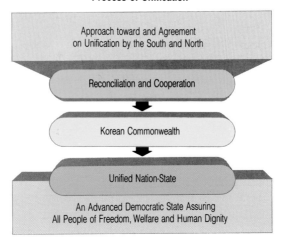

A Phased Process of Unification

The basic philosophy behind the newly-defined policy of building a single Korean national community is rooted in the values of freedom and democracy, which must be defended at any cost. No challenges to freedom and democracy will be tolerated.

The process of unification should be focused on how to ensure that all Koreans will live together, rather than on how to distribute power.

Unification must be based on the values of freedom, democracy and public welfare rather than on any ideology narrowly focused on a specific class or group.

The unification process must be concerned principally with building a single national community in which all Koreans will live together, rather than with developing a hypothetical structure of a unified state.

Principles for Unification

Independence: Unification should be achieved on Korea's own according to the wishes of the Korean people and on the strength of its inherent national capabilities.

Goal of Unification

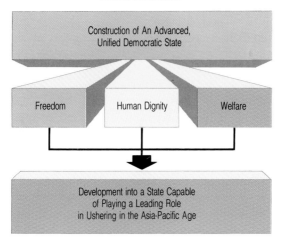

Peace: Unification should be achieved peacefully, not through war or the overthrow of the other side.

Democracy: Unification should be a democratic integration of the nation on the basis of the freedom and rights of all Koreans.

The Unification Process

Unification should be achieved in a gradual and step-by-step basis, with emphasis on building a single national community. To this end, the Korean National Community Unification Formula envisions the following three phases:

Reconciliation and Cooperation: The lingering hostility and distrust between the South and the North which deepened during the Cold War is replaced with a relationship of reconciliation and cooperation.

To this end, the South and the North in this phase must build up mutual trust by recognizing each other's system and energizing multi-pronged exchanges and cooperation as they pledged in the South-North Basic Agreement.

Also in this phase, the two sides would give priority

to resolving humanitarian issues such as arranging the reunion of dispersed families.

Korean Commonwealth: In this phase peaceful coexistence and coprosperity are secured, and the two parts of Korea are joined in a single socio-economic community.

In this phase, the South and the North realize a common national living sphere as an intra-national special relationship, not as state-to-state relations.

Also in this phase the South and the North would jointly establish a council of Presidents and a council of ministers with a view to facilitating ultimate political integration while parliamentary delegates from both sides work out a unified constitution.

Unified Nation-State: A single nation-state is completed by fully integrating the South and North. In this phase the South and the North realize political integration by forming a unified legislature and government under democratic procedures in accordance with the Unified Constitution, thus accomplishing complete unification featuring a single government and system of a single state within one nation.

The Vision of a Unified Korea

The unified Korea sought by the South Korean people is a country that not only cherishes the national tradition and culture but also guarantees each individual's happiness and national prosperity. The basic values that form the basis of this vision are freedom, welfare and human dignity.

The word "freedom" here means that the pain and inconveniences stemming from national division have dissipated; self-rule and the creativity of all people are respected, and political and economic freedom is ensured.

"Welfare" refers to the creation of an affluent economy through the substantial expansion of all of the nation's capacities and the fair distribution of its fruits among all the people.

The phrase "human dignity" means a respect for each individual's inalienable human rights based on statutory order and justice and the end of the human suffering and oppression deriving from the national division.

The unified Korea the Korean people should attain is a single national community in which everyone becomes master, that is, a state where each individual's freedom, welfare and human dignity are ensured, a state which can play a leading role in the coming Asia-Pacific age, and a state contributing to world peace and prosperity.

The North Korean Position

North Korea has constantly insisted upon a unilateral and arbitrary unification formula calling for the creation of a "Koryŏ Democratic Confederation." This formula does not provide for any democratic procedure to reflect the free will of the Korean people, nor does it propose any institutional channel for dialogue. Furthermore, P'yŏngyang has unilaterally defined the name, the form of government and the basic domestic and foreign policies of the proposed confederation.

The so-called "preconditions" for this confederation suggested by North Korea are evidence that it is a mere propaganda ploy. They demand that the current government leadership in Seoul resign and South Korea's anticommunism policies be completely abandoned. They also demand that U.S. troops be withdrawn from Korea.

The North Koreans contradict themselves in this proposal by insisting that the confederation must be based on "mutual recognition and accommodation of different ideologies and political systems in the North and the South." Further, they call for "unified national armed forces," and a "uniform foreign policy." All these run counter to their proposed concept of "confederation," which they define as an "association of states."

The North Koreans assert that intra-Korean exchanges and cooperation should begin only after the proposed confederation has been formed. This is in stark contrast to the South Korean policy of pursuing exchanges and cooperation with the aim of promoting common prosperity, reconciliation and mutual trust to pave the way for peaceful unification.

South and North Korea Today

Since the division of the Korean Peninsula that followed national liberation in 1945, South and North Korea have been guided by totally different ideologies and economic systems. The South adopted a free democratic system and the North rigid communism. The two sides have competed with each other in an attempt to demonstrate the superiority of their respective systems, causing the gap between them to widen.

South Korea, like other liberal democratic countries, endeavors to construct a society guaranteeing public welfare to maintain growth with stability but without inflation, to expand employment opportunities, to distribute the national wealth in a fair way through taxation and social development policies, to promote labor productivity through constant technological innovation, and to increase wages according to individual abilities. On the other hand, in North Korea, because of the contradictory socio-economic system and stagnant light industry, living standards have lagged far behind. It is difficult to compare the living standards of people living in two such entirely different systems, but some indices may be helpful in drawing a rough picture of life in South and North Korea.

South Korea's GNP in 1995 was US$451.7 billion and the per capita GNP reached US$10,076, while North Korea's GNP was US$22.3 billion and its per capita GNP stood at US$957. The South's GNP and per capita GNP were thus 20.3 and 10.5 times those of the North, respectively. This wide gap is primarily attributable to the sustained high growth of the South Korean economy since the 1960s. While the South dealt successfully with the

A "Human Chain'" campaign in support of unification.

two worldwide economic recessions in the '70s, the economy of the North became chronically stagnant due to waste of capital and inefficient investment plans.

The share of military spending in the GNP amounted to 27.2 percent in North Korea in 1994, the second highest in the world after Israel, while that of South Korea was 3.5 percent. Naturally, such excessive military expenditures do not serve a productive cause, but rather stultify growth potential and contribute to economic stagnation. North Korea is being forced to induce Western capital and technology to salvage its faltering economy, which is one of the factors which hopefully may bring it back into a dialogue with the South.

The international stature of South Korea is ever rising due to its economic development and growing national strength. The four superpowers whose interests converge on the Korean Peninsula, the United States, Japan, the People's Republic of China and Russia unanimously want stability on the peninsula and thus support dialogue between Seoul and P'yŏngyang.

Foreign Relations

Background

Although its history spans thousands of years, Korea's wide involvement in international affairs is of recent origin. Traditionally, Korea's external relations were largely confined to immediate neighbors such as China and Japan, with only sporadic contacts with India, Persia and Russia, until the late 19th century when the "Hermit Kingdom" officially opened its doors to the outside world. For centuries, Korea maintained and was greatly influenced by an especially close relationship with China both culturally and politically. However, Korea's contacts with Japan were less cordial, as Japan frequently launched incursions or invasions into the Peninsula.

During the last quarter of the 19th century, Japan was held in check by China and Russia, as the three powers struggled for control over Korea, despite Chosŏn's strenuous efforts to safeguard its independence. However, the balance of power was finally broken by the Sino-Japanese (1894-5) and Russo-Japanese Wars (1904-5), allowing Japan to annex Korea in 1910 and depriving Koreans of their independence for the first time. Japan's colonial rule lasted until 1945, during which time there were vigorous campaigns by patriots at home and abroad to regain independence. Finally, Korea was liberated in the wake of the Allied victory over Japan in World War II. but liberation only led to division along the 38th parallel, in accordance with a wartime agreement between the United States and the Soviet Union.

Korea's relations with the wider world in any significant sense began after the establishment of the Republic in 1948. Even then, external contact started to widen

The 19th Antarctic Treaty Consultative Meeting (ATCM) in Seoul with 250 lawyers, May 8-19, 1995, scientists and government officials from 42 countries attending.

very slowly, beginning with nations having significant interests in Korea. It has only been over the past three decades that the nation's international involvement has become truly global, reflecting its increasing economic strength over that time.

Current Status

The Republic of Korea's diplomacy today focuses on boosting its international contributions and expanding its role on the international stage. Today, the Republic of Korea maintains relations with virtually all countries in the world and actively works to improve cooperative ties with each of them. As of April 1996, the Republic maintains diplomatic relations with 182 nations and keeps 99 embassies, 37 consulates and 5 missions. It is a member of 88 international organizations, including 16 United Nations agencies, and a multitude of nongovernmental international bodies.

Korea is taking a more active role in such international organizations as Unicef.

In the 1990s, the Korean Government has pursued diplomatic policies aimed at securing international support for peace and stability in Northeast Asia, thereby laying the foundation for the unification of the Korean Peninsula. It will also pursue an active economic diplomacy so that the country can join the ranks of the advanced countries, seeking a global role commensurate with its enhanced international standing.

Beyond these essential goals, Korea seeks to achieve economic modernization and to share its experience and expertise with other developing countries. As a country that has benefitted greatly from global free trade, it has tried to run the economy on the principles of mutual cooperation and reciprocity.

Korea is endeavoring to enhance its role in the international community by taking a more active role commensurate with its growing national strength. The 1988 Seoul Olympic Games were a catalyst for the expansion and diversification of international relations. By successfully staging the largest Games in Olympic history up until that point, Koreans contributed to a reconciliation of the East and West and further helped the spread of the ideals of universal harmony and progress.

Traditional Friends

The Republic of Korea Government was established in 1948 through a general election held in accordance with a resolution by the United Nations General Assembly, which then declared that it was the only legitimate government on the Korean Peninsula. During its early years, the Republic looked to the United Nations as the primary arena for its diplomatic efforts. The U.N. General Assembly and the Security Council discussed and passed resolutions on the Korean question every year until the 1970s.

The successive administrations of the Republic tried to uphold the ideals and aims of the United Nations and made determined efforts to obtain full and active membership to better serve the cause of world peace and international cooperation. However, the Republic's efforts to join the world body were stalemated by vetoes exercised by the Soviet Union and China. Successive Korean Governments pursued the goal of the admission of both South and North Korea into the United Nations as an interim arrangement pending unification, in the belief that this would increase opportunities for intra-Korean dialogue and cooperation and expedite the establishment of peace and eventual unification. In September 1991, South Korea's persistent efforts bore fruit as it and North Korea became member states. On becoming U.N. members, South and North Korea pledged to refrain from the use of force against each other and to settle all disputes by peaceful means.

During the early years, when the Republic of Korea faced constant threats to its survival, it concentrated on relations with those countries whose support was vital.

President Kim Young Sam (center) and other leaders take a break from the APEC Leaders Meeting held in Subic, the Philippines, on November 25, 1996.

External relations were therefore primarily directed toward a handful of major powers in the free world. The United States, with its preponderant resources of political, military and economic assistance, played an indispensable role during the formative years of the Republic. It still remains its major ally and largest trading partner. Korea maintains a mutual defense treaty with the United States, which stations some 35,000 troops on the Korean territory as of 1994.

After a complete rupture at the end of World War II, Korea-Japan relations were normalized in 1965. Since then, the two countries have greatly expanded exchanges and cooperation in various fields, but the emotional entanglement of their peoples over past scars has remained a constant challenge for the foreign policymakers of both countries.

The Republic of Korea established diplomatic relations

with the Soviet Union in 1990. Since the fall of the Soviet Union, Korea has developed cordial and cooperative relations with Russia. Since Korea established diplomatic relations with China in 1992, Korea-China bilateral relations have expanded rapidly in all areas to the extent that two-way trade reached the level of US$17 billion in 1995.

Korea has maintained friendly relations with the European Union and the other countries of Europe. Bilateral relations with individual European nations continue to be of considerable importance in political, economic, cultural and other areas. A closer and mutually advantageous relationship with the EU is also being pursed.

The New Administration's Foreign Policy

President Kim Young Sam enunciated Korea's New Diplomacy on May 24, 1993. Its basic goals are to promote the universal values of democracy, human dignity and market economies, to help build the 21st century into an era of peaceful coexistence and global prosperity, and to play an ever broader role in the international arena. This diplomacy is intended to be in line with the ROK's overall globalization policy. Accordingly, Korea will actively contribute to world peace by participating in U.N. peacekeeping operations and by taking a more prominent role in the promotion of regional peace and prosperity. It also seeks to promote multilateral dialogue on regional security in the Asia-Pacific region, and as a founding member of APEC, has actively participated in the APEC process in order to promote progress and prosperity within the region. It will also strengthen its participation in the workings of the WTO, thus contributing to a new world trade order. Korea will also share the benefits of its developmental experience and technology with other developing nations.

Also high on the agenda of Korean diplomacy is how to tackle the North Korean nuclear threat. South Korea believes that a successful settling of this issue will contribute to peace and stability on the Korean Peninsula and lead to a peaceful unification of the country.

The Republic seeks to base its relations with other countries on shared values. Its relationship with the United States, which was dominated in the past chiefly by a military alliance, is being developed into a mature political, economic and social partnership on the basis of common values and ideals. Nevertheless, Seoul wants Washington to maintain its military presence in Korea until a lasting peace is established on the Korean Peninsula. The Republic will also try to ameliorate its relations with Japan, which have, at times, been strained by an antagonistic past, by emphasizing practical interests and a prosperous future. Diplomatic efforts will also be directed at developing mutually advantageous partnerships with Russia and China.

The country will also actively participate in international endeavors to address such global issues as the deteriorating environment, population control, narcotics traffic, terrorism, and human rights. It will expand and strengthen its role in the United Nations and other international organizations. Its membership in the Organization for Economic Cooperation and Development (OECD), which was realized in 1996, will contribute to the expansion of free and open trade in the world, not to mention Korea's own continued development.

Economy

Phenomenal Growth

Over the last three decades, the Republic of Korea has achieved what is widely acclaimed as "the economic miracle on the Han-gang River." Since Korea embarked on economic development in earnest in 1962, its economy has grown at one of the fastest paces in the world. As a result, Korea, long one of the world's poorest agrarian societies, has emerged as an upper middle-income, fast-industrializing country.

In around three decades, from 1962 to 1995, Korea's gross national product increased from US $2.3 billion to US $451.7 billion, with per capita GNP soaring from US $87 to about US $10,076 at current price levels. The key to this success was the adoption of an outward-looking development strategy making exports the engine of growth—a strategy that reflected Korea's insufficient natural endowments, its limited domestic market, and its abundant, well-educated, industrious manpower.

The economic structure was radically transformed as a result of the successful development programs implemented during these years. The manufacturing sector increased its share of GDP from 14.4 percent to over 26.9 percent in 1995. The commodity trade volume reached more than US $260.2 billion in 1995 in contrast to US $477 million in 1962. The gross savings ratio rose to 36.2 percent from 11.0 percent during the same period.

Korea's development is even more remarkable in view of its situation until the early 1960s. Korea had been economically backward for most of its long history. There

The steel industry has been a backbone of Korea's economic development. The Pohang Iron and Steel Company is the world's second biggest steel company.

were few significant industries before liberation from Japan's 35-year colonial rule (1910-45), during which Korea's economic resources were ruthlessly exploited by the Japanese. The Korean economy was further devastated during the Communist-provoked Korean War (1950-1953), the damage from which took a long time to heal. As late as 1961, Korea was still suffering from the many difficulties commonly faced by less developed nations. On top of its extreme poverty, the population was growing by 3 percent annually. Unemployment prevailed and savings were negligible. The nation had no notable exports, and it depended on imports for both raw materials and important manufactured goods.

Industrial Development

Given the limited size of the domestic market, economic planners found it necessary to adopt an export-oriented industrialization strategy. This outward-development strategy was particularly well suited to Korea's conditions in the early 1960s. Government in-

Korea has become one of the world's top shipmakers. In 1995, Korea received orders for over 7.1 million G/T. of ship construction.

itiatives played an important part in development efforts. A more realistic single exchange rate was adopted and short-term export financing was made available. Customs procedures were simplified, enabling exporters to easily import necessary raw materials. Foreign investment was also strongly encouraged.

The First Five-Year Economic Development Plan (1962-66) focused on laying a foundation for industrialization and was successful in initiating and accelerating a structural readjustment of industry from subsistence agriculture to modern manufacturing and export trade. The share of primary industries in the overall industrial structure decreased from 34.8 percent in 1966 to 23.5 percent in 1976 and to 6.6 percent in 1995. On the other hand, the share of secondary industries increased from 20.5 percent in 1966 to 27.2 percent in 1995. Tertiary industries held their ground, with a total share of 66.2 percent in 1995 compared with 44.7 percent in 1966.

In the initial stage of industrialization, labor-intensive light industry, especially textiles, was the growth lead-

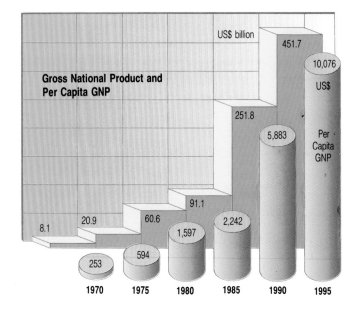

Gross National Product and Per Capita GNP

US$ billion

Year	GNP (US$ billion)	Per Capita GNP (US$)
1970	8.1	253
1975	20.9	594
1980	60.6	1,597
1985	91.1	2,242
1990	251.8	5,883
1995	451.7	10,076

er, but more recently, the rapidly developing heavy and chemical industries have come to account for over half of the nation's total manufacturing output. Korea became the 6th largest steel producer in the world with the completion of the third Kwang Yang Blast Furnace in December, 1990.

The country is also developing the production of a wide range of industrial machinery and equipment. The electronics industry is another major growth sector, and an increasingly important foreign exchange earner. While the ship-building industry has already passed its peak, car manufacturing is seeing a boom with soaring demands in both the local and overseas markets.

Two large petrochemical complexes have been developed to meet increasing domestic demand. They are supported by several large refineries located along the three coasts of the country. Other principal industrial products include cement, processed foods, plywood, chemical fertilizers, footwear, ceramics, glass, nonferrous

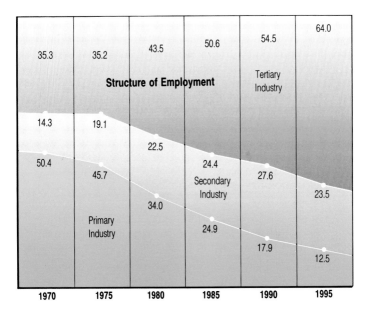

	1970	1975	1980	1985	1990	1995
Tertiary Industry	35.3	35.2	43.5	50.6	54.5	64.0
Secondary Industry	14.3	19.1	22.5	24.4	27.6	23.5
Primary Industry	50.4	45.7	34.0	24.9	17.9	12.5

Structure of Employment

metals and farm implements.

Overall agricultural production doubled in the 15 years following the launching of the First Five-Year Economic Development Plan in 1962. Growth has since slowed, but the much emphasized goal of self-sufficiency in rice, the staple food of Korea, has been attained with an output of 4.70 million tons in 1995.

Agricultural development efforts have been concentrated mainly on maximizing yields from the country's limited arable land—only 20 percent of total land area in 1995. New high-yield varieties of rice and other crops have been introduced. A large fertilizer and pesticide industry has been developed to keep farmers adequately supplied with these products.

There has been a rapid growth in fruits, vegetables and other high-value cash crops, and in livestock products, the demand for which has been increasing rapidly in tune with rising income levels. The spread of vinyl greenhouses has been a major factor in the increased size of the vegetable harvest which, in the 1980s, helped the average farm household to catch up with the average urban working family in terms of annual income. This equilibrium is maintained today.

The farm population has steadily decreased in accordance with the progress of industrialization. The percentage of rural residents in the national population dropped from 57 percent in 1962 to a mere 11 percent in 1995. Great efforts have been made for farm mechanization to solve the problem of the shortage of rural labor. Mechanization has progressed most in the planting and harvesting of rice.

A nationwide reforestation movement has been in force since the early 1970s to drape in green the once denuded hills of the country, which account for some 66 percent of the total land area. Vigorous measures are being taken annually to plant a large number of trees, nurse newly planted ones and protect older ones, while new varieties that are more productive and more resistant to pests and disease are being developed.

To conserve forest resources until they become fully productive, tree cutting is strictly controlled. For over a decade, timber production has been held to around one million cubic meters, and the annual production of firewood and charcoal limited to less than five million tons. Much of the timber demand has been met by imports. These efforts have greatly contributed to flood and soil erosion control as well.

The expansion and modernization of Korea's fishing industry has been remarkable over the past two decades, making it an important source of foreign exchange earnings. The fish catch increased rapidly as modern, motorized vessels began to operate in coastal waters as well as in the deep seas. Korean fishing bases have been established in Western Samoa and Las Palmas and consumers now enjoy cuttlefish caught in waters off the Falkland Islands.

The deep-sea catch from the seven seas reached a peak

Korea's trade volume has inceased at an unprecedented pace.

in the middle of the 1970s and then fell significantly due to rising fuel costs and the declaration of 200-mile economic sea zones by many nations. Korea has negotiated fishing agreements with a number of coastal nations to secure fishing rights in their economic waters and is continuing efforts to prop up the deep-sea fishing industry, which began to recover a few years ago.

Market Liberalization

Deregulation of imports began in the middle of the 1970s with selected manufactured goods. The deregulation process accelerated after 1983, and now covers a wide range of goods and services, including agricultural products and finance. Tariffs have been abolished or reduced, and such non-tariff barriers as domestic regulatory laws relaxed.

By the middle of 1987, the second consecutive year that Korea had registered a current accounts surplus, the government became convinced that the black ink was structural rather than transitory. Efforts were thus

Exports and Imports by Commodity Group

(In million U.S. dollars)

Items	Exports		Imports	
	1985	1995	1985	1995
Total	**30,283**	**125,058**	**31,136**	**135,119**
Food and live animals	1,136	2,656	1,398	5,926
Crude materials, inedible, except fuels	298	1,790	3,857	11,713
Mineral fuels, lubricants and related materials	951	2,472	7,363	19,103
Chemicals and related products	936	8,944	2,789	13,156
Manufactured goods	15,436	40,750	4,787	32,074
Machinery and transport equipment	11,384	65,646	10,648	49,436
Others	142	2,800	294	3,711

deemed necessary to reduce surpluses in the current account, which the government sought to do by promoting a "balanced expansion of trade."

Consistent with its commitment to free trade principles, Korea initiated ambitious steps to open its markets. These steps involved a streamlining of import procedures, slashed tariffs, strengthened protection of foreign-based intellectual property rights and better access to Korea's services sector.

Since the automatic license approval system was abolished on January 1, 1997, virtually all manufactured goods, with very few exceptions, can be imported into Korea by reporting to the Customs Office. Thus, imports to Korea are almost completely liberalized. The overall liberalization ratio reached 99.3 percent in 1996, close to that of many development countries.

Tariffs Slashed

Korea embarked on an extensive five-year tariff reduction program in 1984. The tariff rate (average) for manufactured goods was cut in half—from 22.6 percent in 1983 to 6.2 percent in 1996. A figure comparable to that of many OECD countries including Canada (7.3

An increasing variety of foreign products are now on sale in Korea thanks to import liberalization.

percent), the European Union (6.7 percent) and the United States (6.1 percent).

Also down substantially is the general tariff rate. It dropped from 23.7 percent on average in 1983 to 7.9 percent in 1996.

Average tariff rates for agricultural goods dropped from 31.4 percent in 1983 to 16.6 percent in 1996.

Import Procedures Streamlined

Invisible trade barriers can be a significant obstacle to free trade. Thus an essential element of Korea's moves toward market openness have included a simplification of import procedures. "Individual laws" designed to regulate imported goods from a health and safety standpoint are being moderated and in many cases rescinded. The restrictions under individual laws will be brought into conformity with GATT provisions, in line with the results of the UR.

In July 1988, local content requirements in government procurement were abolished. Korea has joined the WTO Agreement on Government Procurement.

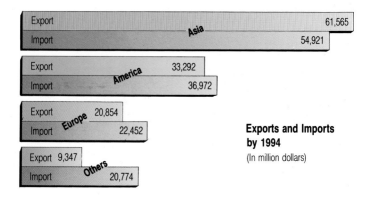

**Exports and Imports
by 1994**
(In million dollars)

Services Sector

Liberalization of Korea's services sector has been difficult due to the relatively underdeveloped state of domestic service industries. Nevertheless the government has taken a number of unilateral actions toward its eventual full opening. To cite some examples, the life insurance market is now completely open to foreign underwriters. Foreign banks receive treatment commensurate to that of national banks. Investment by foreigners in trading and wholesaling is also open, although restrictions exist in specific areas. The advertising market, once open only to joint ventures with minority foreign participation, is now completely accessible to foreigners.

Intellectual Property Rights

The government recognizes that strong intellectual property right protection is essential for the technological well-being of Korea and for stable economic relations with major trading partners. Consequently since 1987 it has instituted fundamental reforms to strengthen the protection of intellectual property. Korea's new copyright law stipulates comprehensive protection for both foreign and domestic works. Copyright guarantee extends to the life of an author plus fifty years. Safeguards

Agricultural products imported from all over the world are available at most supermarkets.

against intellectual property infringement have been extended to computer software through specific legislation.

Agricultural Market Moves Toward Openness

In Korea, as in the United States, the European Union and Japan, agricultural policy is fraught with far-reaching social and political implications, which make it a difficult sector to liberalize. Domestic agriculture accounts for 6.6 percent of Korea's GNP and nearly 12.5 percent of total employment in 1995—in stark contrast to the U.S. figures of 2.1 percent and 3.2 percent respectively. Korean sensitivity about agriculture derives in part from the fact that arable land per farmer is only 1/223 that of the U.S.

However, Korean Government is making efforts to further open the agricultural market. These efforts are accompanied by continuing government initiatives to further open the agricultural market. The government formed a task force in December 1988 to revise the schedules for agricultural import liberalization through 1991. The revised plans have helped to increase the scope of liberalization and accelerate the pace of opening. Also, in the Uruguay Round's negotiation on the agricultural products, we has committed to improving the market access for various agricultural products.

Science and Technology

Another major area that has received top priority is science and technology. Because of the changing global situation, Korea's competitive edge in labor-intensive industries such as textiles, footwear, and parts assembly has been eroding. In these industries, Korea is facing much tougher competition from other developing countries. On the other hand, in trying to move into the high-growth technology market, it meets formidable challenges posed by the increasingly rapid technological advances being made by industrialized countries.

With little choice but to upgrade industry, the government has emphasized accelerated development of science and technology as the basis for industrial restructuring. A major step toward that end was taken in January 1982 with the establishment of the Science and Technology Promotion Council, chaired by the president. Other measures taken included upgrading the Korea Institute of Science and Technology (KIST), the Korea Advanced Institute of Science and Technology (KAIST) and the Daedŏk Science Town near Taejŏn, among other science research institutes. KIST and KAIST have played a vital role in the advancement of scientific knowledge and technological expertise. The Daedŏk Science Town was completed in November 1992, and 60 research and development institutions and three universities are located there. Steps have also been taken to train scientists, engineers and technicians, while inducing talented Korean scientists educated and trained in advanced foreign countries to return home.

As of 1994, there were 2,640 R&D related institutions in Korea, which included 217 public research institutes, 244 at universities, colleges and junior colleges, and 2,179 belonging to private enterprises. The total R&D investment increased from a mere 0.81 percent of GNP in 1981 to 2.61 percent in 1994, or 9.9 billion U.S. dollars. It will rise to 4 percent in 1998 and more than 5 percent by the year 2001, thus narrowing the gap with the major industrialized countries. A package of tax and credit incentives has been provided to help firms raise their research activities to 3-4 percent of gross sales, a level comparable to that prevailing in the advanced countries.

The priority areas for intensive R&D activities range from computers, semiconductors and robotics to telecommunications and fine chemicals. In the long run, Korea will intensify R&D activities for the development of new materials, bio technology, alternative energy sources, and oceanographic and aeronautic technologies. The ultimate aim is to boost Korea's technical level so that it will be able to join the ranks of the world's 7 most technologically advanced countries.

New Challenges and Future Prospects

The Korean economy, which successfully recovered from a deep recession in the wake of the second oil shock, continued a rapid pace of noninflationary growth under conditions of stability until 1988.

However, from 1989, the Korean economy started to experience difficulties, including slower growth, high inflation and a deterioration in the balance of payments.

The GNP growth rate fell to 6.9 percent in 1989 from the 8.4 percent level of previous years. A slump in the growth rate of the manufacturing sector, from 20.1 percent in 1987 and 13.4 percent in 1988 to 5.1 percent in 1992 contributed to the declining GNP growth. The export growth rate, which was 36.2 percent in 1987 and 28.4 percent in 1988, fell to just 6.6 percent in 1992.

In light of these economic difficulties, President Kim Young Sam at the start of his presidential term designated the creation of a New Economy as his top priority in the overall effort to create a New Korea. In order to revitalize the economy, the new economic policy is intended to foster private initiative and creativity at all levels of business and free the economy from the constricting government planning and intervention characteristic of the past three decades.

Following the implementation of the 100-Day Plan for the New Economy in early 1993, the Korean government formally announced its Five-Year Plan for the New Economy in June 1993. If the plan is implemented as scheduled, the Korean economy is projected to achieve an average annual growth rate of 7% between 1994 and 1998, and its per capital GNP is expected to reach U.S.$14,000 by the end of 1998. The plan also seeks to achieve a balance of payments surplus, thereby becoming a net creditor, as well as economic stability with an annual average consumer price increase of 3 percent.

The Five-Year Plan for the New Economy attempts to secure the growth potential of the Korean economy by improving the overall competitiveness of the economy. Industrial competitiveness is to be strengthened through the structural adjustment of industries, technological innovations, improvement of information networks, and the enforcement of fair competition rules. For instance, small-and medium-sized firms, as well as the agriculture and fishery industries, are to become more competitive through the structural adjustment process. The Plan also emphasizes the expansion of social overhead capital, the improvement of labor relations, and the promotion of the efficient use of human and other resources.

Internationalization of the Korean economy is another key ingredient of the Five-Year Plan. As such, the Plan is designed to promote transparency in trade-related government policies and regulations, to improve the domestic investment environment, to undertake step by step liberalization (particularly in the agriculture, services and financial sectors), and to upgrade domestic economic practices to meet international standards. The internationalization attempt will also help modernize the domestic economy.

After the economic slowdown in 1991-1993, the Korean economy appears to be in steady recovery. The GNP growth rate recorded a robust 8.7% in 1995, while industrial production grew at 9.1% per annum in the same year. As the economy recovers, the employment situation has also improved. The unemployment rate declined to 2.1% in 1995 from 3.1% in 1993. Despite the economic recovery, price stability does not appear to be at risk. Consumer prices rose by a modest 4.5% per annum in 1995.

The recent globalization attempt will cultivate Korea's efforts to achieve the New Economy. With a successful completion of globalization efforts, an educational system where youngsters with creative minds and enterprising spirits are fostered and where self-discipline and competitiveness are emphasized will be established to strengthen Korea's intellectual potential. A free market order based on fair competition will dictate all economic activities; all economic transactions will be carried out in a more transparent and fairer environment, more competition will be introduced in the financial market, and factors of production will be allowed to move across borders without interruption. Government activities will be geared towards providing public service to the private sector, and a dramatic deregulation of administrative procedures will be implemented to achieve a "small and efficient" government. Ways of thought and behavior will be changed in such a way that Korean people will cooperate with the rest of the world.

Social Welfare

Employment

Due to rapid economic growth and the improved industrial structure achieved during the past three decades, the problem of unemployment has virtually been overcome in Korea. In fact, manpower shortages began occurring in some industrial sectors during a boom period in the late '70s, suggesting that the Korean economy no longer enjoyed an unlimited manpower supply.

In 1963, the second year of the First Five-Year Economic Development Plan, the unemployment rate was a fairly high 8.2 percent, with the number of employed totaling 7.7 million. Rural employment accounted for 63 percent of this total employment, indicating a considerably high rate of unemployment in urban areas. However, the employment picture has since improved steadily, with a substantial number of rural workers having moved into manufacturing and service sectors created by the country's rapid industrialization.

The unemployment rate stood at 2.0 percent in 1995, but it is generally agreed that the economy will no longer benefit from an unlimited work force. The percentage of those employed in mining and manufacturing stood at 23.5, and those in services at 64.0. Employment in agriculture, forestry and fisheries plummeted to 12.5 percent, about 35 percent of the level of the early 1960s.

In order to train technical manpower and expand employment in preparation for the advent of an advanced industrial society, Korea's manpower development programs emphasize the better utilization of educated or trained manpower, the improvement of working con-

Status of Employed

Unit: 1,000 persons

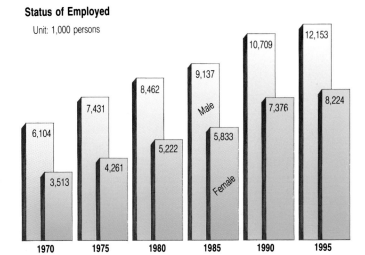

	1970	1975	1980	1985	1990	1995
Male	6,104	7,431	8,462	9,137	10,709	12,153
Female	3,513	4,261	5,222	5,833	7,376	8,224

ditions, the encouragement of constructive dialogue between labor and management, and the revitalization of labor unions. To increase employment opportunities, emphasis has been put on the development of skilled labor intensive industries and on increasing scientists and technicians through expansion of vocational and technical education. In-house training by industries has also been encouraged.

In light of the rapidly-changing economic realities, the Government has revised labor-related statutes as part of its economic reform. The revisions target working conditions, such as wages and working hours, the activities of labor unions and the dispute-resolution system. The Government has provided the foundation for establishing rational interaction between labor and management through a joint commission composed of laborers and employers. Furthermore, the employment insurance system was established as of July 1995, administering four social security systems: employment insurance, the national pension system, medical insurance and workmen's compensation insurance.

More and more apartment complexes are including parks and green areas
as people want healthier and more spacious living environments.

Housing

A chronic housing shortage persists in Korea due to a sharp rise in housing demands fueled by the continuous population expansion, the move toward nuclear families and the heavy migration to cities. Overpopulation and spiraling land prices in large cities, in particular, have led to an imbalance in housing distribution between urban and rural areas. As of 1995, the housing supply ratio stood at 86.1 percent.

In order to solve the housing problem and stabilize housing costs, the supply of land available for construction and the building of small housing units has continuously been emphasized. Beginning in 1988, the Government had established and promoted the Two Million Housing Unit Construction Plan for the period 1988-1992 with a view to reestablishing a balance in housing demand and supply.

Construction performance for the period 1988-1992 reached 2,717,000 units, exceeding the target of

2,000,000 units. This rapid increase in housing supply relieved the shortage problem in urban areas and contributed to stabilizing sharply rising housing prices.

The Government plans to continuously supply, on average, 500,000 to 600,000 housing units per year from 1993 to 1997, thereby increasing the housing supply ratio to 100% in 2005.

The Government's housing construction projects, carried out by the Korea Housing Corporation, and financial subsidies to private enterprises will continue to focus on small housing units even after the completion of the Two Million Housing Unit Construction Plan.

The piped water system has continuously been expanded to ensure more sanitary living conditions. The supply of tap water will be boosted from 67 percent in 1985 to 83 percent in 1995 and 90 percent in 2001 through the current water development project. The per capita amount of water supplied will also be raised from the 282 liters in 1985 to 398 liters in 1995 and 440 liters in 2001. If the water development project goes ahead as scheduled, running tap water will reach 90 percent of households, including all rural villages, by the first year of the next century.

Health and Medical Services

The health of the Korean people as a whole has improved substantially. This is directly related to the improvement of diet, the rise in living standards and the development of health and medical programs, all prompted by the rapid economic growth since the 1970s. The life expectancy at birth was 73.5 as of 1995 and child mortality before the age of four was 12.1 per 1,000 births in 1994.

The rate of infection by communicable and other diseases has gradually declined, though the loss of manpower caused by illnesses remains significant. The incidence of tuberculosis has declined remarkably and the rate of parasite infection has also dropped to a low 0.5 percent as of 1991. From the early 1980s, outbreaks of cholera and encephalitis have been virtually eradicated.

People are using medicine with growing frequency, and the share of medical costs in total household expenditures has increased accordingly. In 1963, the medical expenses of an urban family averaged 2,280 won ($2.78) per year or 2.7 percent of total spending and that of a rural family 1,893 won ($2.31) or 2.4 percent. In 1995, however, this average jumped to 747,600 won per year or 4.8 percent of an urban family budget.

Since the latter half of the 1970s, medical security, in the form of medical insurance and medical aid, has been expanded to cover a substantial portion of the population. As of 1995, the total number of people benefiting from medical insurance and aid were 44,016,000 and 1,989,600 persons, respectively. The coverage was only 29.5 percent in 1980. The national medical insurance system was expanded on July 1, 1989 to cover a substantial portion of the population, and now more than 95.3 percent of the people has access to health insurance, with the remaining 4.7 percent being able to receive

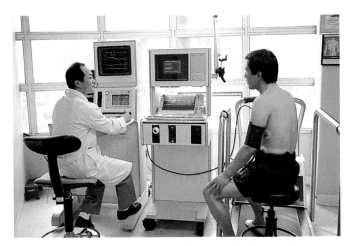

Periodic checkups are conducted under the national medical insurance plan.

direct medical aid.

Korea's medical supply system and medical resources are still insufficient in general to meet the sharply rising medical needs engendered by the advancement of the medical security system. For instance, 1995 statistics showed that there was one physician for 784 persons and one hospital bed for every 230 persons. In order to supply low-cost, quality medicine to all people, therefore, efforts are being made to establish an effective medical supply system through reasonable distribution and supply of medical resources. To ensure the qualitative improvement of health and medical programs, more effective means of hospital management are being pursued.

Among the major projects currently under way to enhance the public health and medical insurance systems are a restructuring of the countrywide medical network so as to establish primary health care posts under the existing health centers; the early detection and control of such communicable diseases as tuberculosis and leprosy, and the provision of free treatment to sufferers thereof; the establishment and operation of special examination centers for mental disorders; and active public education on the need for early examination and treatment of all health problems. Other projects in support of these same goals include nutritional improvement for those in low-income brackets; establishment of mother-child health clinics to further reduce maternal and infant mortality, the promotion of large and more up-to-date food processing industries, and the subsidizing of a private food inspection center and a training institute for food and sanitary guidance workers.

As of December 1995, medical institutions participating in medical insurance programs numbered 53,674 across the country. They included 266 general hospitals, 462 hospitals, 14 dental hospitals, 14,569 clinics, 8,363 dental clinics and 183 maternity clinics. With 70 herb doctor hospitals, 5,743 herb doctor clinics, oriental herbal medicine has been included in the medical insurance program since 1987.

Social Security

The living standards of the Korean people have substantially improved owing to the rapid economic growth during the past couple of decades. Because of such growth, however, Korean society has had to undergo in a short period the kind of changes that took place in the developed countries of the West over several centuries. This has caused numerous socio-economic problems, including the disintegration of traditional values, a widespread sense of relative poverty and other difficulties accompanying industrialization, urbanization and the breakup of the traditional extended family.

The Korean Government, keenly conscious of these circumstances, has adopted the building of a society capable of ensuring the well-being of the entire population as a major national goal. The Constitution contains provisions to guarantee the welfare of all citizens. Various laws have been enacted to promote the welfare of the handicapped and the aged and to establish a social welfare fund. To help needy families stand on their own feet, a self-help program has been instituted to provide them with assistance in education and vocational training and with small business loans, in addition to subsistence aid. Institutes to accommodate those 65 or older, the handicapped, under-privileged youth, unmarried mothers and fatherless families are continuously being expanded.

In Korea, however, the history of modern social security dates only to 1963, when the Social Security Law was enacted. The key devices provided by this law fall into two categories: various social insurance payments and public relief programs. The first category is comprised of medical, business suspension, unemployment, old age, industrial accident, family allowance, child delivery and bereaved family and funeral payments. Public relief activities in the form of subsistence, income support and medical care are extended to the needy and feeble, such as the elderly and those disabled due to injury, mental derangement or physical handicaps.

A pension system introduced in 1988 was expanded to cover all work places and the self-employed. But persons working at work places having 4 or fewer employees and the self-employed, excluding farmers and fishermen, are insured on a voluntary basis with their premium being determined by their average wage level. The others are insured compulsorily.

The national pension system covers nearly all risks for those with benefits, including a retirement pension, work-related accident benefits, a survivor pension and lump-sum payments, except for civil servants, military personnel and private school teachers, who are covered by their own pension program.

As of the end of 1995, the number of people covered by the national pension system reached 7,257,000.

Women

In traditional Korean society, women were largely confined to the home. From a young age, women were required to learn the Confucian virtues of subordination and endurance to prepare for their future roles as wife and mother, while being denied any opportunity to participate in activities outside the home. Their role was limited to the management of the large extended family and the producing of a male heir so that the family line might continue unbroken.

The situation began to improve, however, thanks to the education of women which followed the opening of the country to the outside world during the late 19th century. Educated women engaged in the arts, teaching and religious work, as well as the enlightenment of other women. The self-awakening of women led to the awakening of their national consciousness and patriotism under the Japanese occupation. Women took part in the independence movement with no less vigor, determination and courage than men. A women's liberation movement calling for expanded rights also began to emerge.

With the establishment of the Republic in 1948, women achieved the clear constitutional right to equal education and job opportunities and to participate in public life. A growing number of parents came to believe that their daughters needed to get as much education as their sons. Society in general grew increasingly understanding toward working women, while it is also true that it needed the work of the female population for industrialization.

A series of successful economic development plans has helped Korea achieve remarkable economic growth and social transformation. Women have had increasingly greater opportunities to take part in economic activities. Export-oriented industries in particular have come to require a large female labor force. As of 1995, there were

An increasing number of Korean women are pursuing professional careers.

Distribution of Employed Women by Occupation (1995) Unit: 1,000

Items	Total (A)	Female (B)	Female Ratio (B/A: %)
Legislators, senior officials & managers	525	23	4.4
Professionals, technicians & associate professionals	2,811	896	31.9
Clerks	2,510	1,277	50.9
Service workers & market sales workers	4,464	2,631	58.9
Skilled agricultural & fishery workers	2,389	1,110	46.5
Craft & related trades workers	3,219	787	24.4
Plant, machine operators & assemblers	2,175	309	14.2
Elementary occupations	2,284	1,191	52.1
Total	20,377	8,224	40.4

8.2 million working women who accounted for 40.4 percent of the total work force. Despite this increase, the number of women holding policy making positions in administration and management is still very small.

Korean women today, however, are actively engaged in a wide variety of fields including education, medicine, science, engineering, scholarship, arts, literature and sports. There are female lawmakers, business executives and university presidents. Though only a handful in number, some women have proved their excellent abilities and leadership as cabinet ministers. These all attest to the fact that Korean women, given opportunities, can develop their potential and make significant contributions to society.

The increasing role of women and the changes in Korean society as a whole have brought the government to the realization that it must develop new policies for women. By a presidential decree, the National Committee on Women's Policies was formed in 1983 with representatives of the concerned government ministries. The Korean Women's Development Institute was established in the same year to make a comprehensive study of women's issues and link its findings with actual policies.

Today, the portion of social participation by women in various walks of life increases every year in Korea. In compliance with the changing social environment, the government established the Ministry of Political Affairs (2) to handle women's matters in 1988. Not surprisingly, the government named a female minister to lead. In the same year, 15 Family Welfare Bureaus with women directors were also established at the provincial government level. In addition, in 1991, 274 Family Welfare Divisions with female chiefs in towns, counties and wards were also founded to deal with women's welfare issues.

On June 25, 1994, a Special Committee on Women was established at the National Assembly as permanent body to discuss and legislate laws related to women.

As of April 1995, there were two women in cabinet, serving as the Minister of Political Affairs (2) and the Minister of Education.

Women's roles in society have expanded to the highest decision-making levels. Suggestions by various women's organizations are reflected in policy decisions following the increase in the number of highly educated women as well as the social movement toward sexual equality.

Education

Koreans generally attach great importance to education. This was true for many centuries when the state examination was the main venue for recruiting government officials. Success in the examination was the most honorable and surest road to success. In modern Korea, education is still considered to be of prime importance because it produces the manpower needed for economic and technological advancement.

It was in the 1880s, with the opening of Korea to the outside world, that the first modern schools were established, many of them by Western Christian missionaries. However, the development of a modern education system was soon interrupted by Japan's colonial rule (1910-45) and the Korean War (1950-53). The educational system and opportunities have expanded with remarkable speed since then. Today Korea boasts one of the highest literacy rates in the world, and its well-educated people are regarded as the primary resource for the impressive national development achieved in recent years.

The Ministry of Education is the central government organization responsible for the formulation and implementation of policies related to academic activities, the sciences and public education. The provinces and special cities have boards of education which function as representative bodies. Under these boards are educational commissioners for each county and city who are responsible for educational activities in primary, middle and high schools. The government advises them on basic policy matters and provides financial assistance.

The financing of education is centralized, and government grants constitute the largest component of school

budgets. The budget of the Ministry of Education varies from year to year, but generally accounts for some 22.7 percent of the total government outlay, about 3.84 percent of GNP in 1995.

Preschool education is not compulsory but the six years of primary school have been free and compulsory since 1953. Compulsory education was expanded to three-year middle schools in rural areas in 1992, with the goal of expanding it throughout the country in the near future.

The importance of preschool education has been drawing increasing recognition in recent years. As of 1996, 551,770 children three to five years of age were enrolled in 8,939 kindergartens across the nation. The Ministry of Education has worked out a long-term development plan for the education of pre-school children, calling for an increase in kindergarten facilities so that up to 90 percent of all children of kindergarten age can be admitted by 2005.

Education System

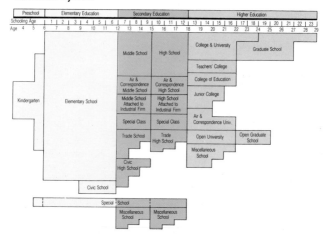

| Preschool | Elementary Education | Secondary Education | Higher Education |

Schooling Age 1 2 3 4 5 6 7 8 9 10 11 12 13 14 15 16 17 18 19 20 21 22 23
Age 4 5 6 7 8 9 10 11 12 13 14 15 16 17 18 19 20 21 22 23 24 25 26 27 28 29

Kindergarten — Elementary School — Middle School — High School — College & University — Graduate School — Teachers' College — College of Education — Junior College — Air & Correspondence Middle School — Air & Correspondence High School — Middle School Attached to Industrial Firm — High School Attached to Industrial Firm — Air & Correspondence Univ. — Special Class — Trade School — Trade High School — Open University — Open Graduate School — Miscellaneous School — Civic High School — Civic School — Special School — Miscellaneous School

The School System

Korea's education system consists of six-year elementary schools, three-year middle schools, three-year high schools and four-year colleges or universities with graduate courses leading to Ph.D. degrees. There are also two-year junior colleges and vocational colleges.

There were 5,732 elementary schools in 1996, enrolling 3,800,540 pupils in 106,594 classes and staffed by 137,912 teachers. The basic elementary school curriculum is composed of nine principal subjects: moral education, Korean language, social studies, mathematics, science, physical education, music, fine arts and practical arts. In the first and second grades, some of these subjects are taught in combined courses and practical arts are added from the third grade. The completion of four-year courses of study at teacher's college is required for elementary school teachers.

Upon completing elementary school, children in the 12-14 age bracket are allowed to enter middle school for the seventh to ninth grade courses. The percentage of elementary school graduates advancing to middle

school has increased remarkably during the past two decades, from 61.8 percent in 1969 to 99.1 percent in 1996. There were 2,705 middle schools with a total enrollment of 2,739,983 students in Korea as of 1996.

Since the abolition of middle school entrance examinations in 1969, assignment to middle schools has been made through a lottery administered on a zone basis, which allows the applicants no choice. The change was aimed at removing distinctions between superior and inferior schools, and thereby equalizing the quality of education provided by all middle schools and relieving children from the pressures of entrance examinations.

The middle school curriculum consists of 11 basic or required subjects, a number of elective subjects, and extracurricular activities. Technical and vocational courses are included in the elective subjects for those who may seek employment after graduation.

The high school entrance system was revised in 1974 to effect a lottery assignment on a zone basis for applicants who passed the qualifying state examination. The revision, which abolished examinations administered by individual schools, was designed to equalize high school education. It resulted in increasing the number of middle school graduates advancing to high school.

The total high school enrollment in 1996 stood at 2,243,307 in 1,847 schools employing a total of 101,591 teachers and instructors. High schools are largely divided into two categories, academic and vocational. As of 1996, there were a total of 771 vocational high schools.

Applicants for vocational high schools must be middle school graduates. They must take a preliminary examination which is administered at the provincial level. The curriculum of these schools is usually 40–60 percent general courses and 60–40 percent vocational courses which place equal emphasis on theory and practice.

There are a number of different kinds of institutions of higher learning in Korea: colleges and universities with four-year undergraduate programs (six years for medical and dental colleges), four-year teacher's colleges, two-year junior vocational colleges, the air and correspondence university and open universities and miscellaneous schools of collegiate status with two- or four-year courses such as nursing schools and theological seminaries.

As of 1996, there were 336 institutions of higher learning in Korea. They include 164 colleges and universities attended by a total of 1,735,887 students and 152 junior vocational colleges with a total enrollment of 642,697 students. About 80 percent of these institutes are private.

In accordance with the Education Law and relevant decrees, all institutes of higher learning, whether public or private, come under the supervision of the Ministry of Education. The ministry exercises control over such matters as student quotas, qualifications of the teaching staff, curriculum and degree requirements and general courses.

Colleges and universities in Korea operate under strict

The main gate of Seoul National University also serves as a university symbol.

enrollment limits. Because of the difference in admission quotas and the number of applicants, each school year produces a large number of repeat applicants, adding to the competitiveness. The college entrance system has undergone drastic reform since 1981. A new system was introduced in 1993 which combines the student's high school academic achievements and his or her score on a nationwide qualifying examination to determine the applicant's eligibility for admission. A few universities and colleges, less than 10, still require an additional entrance examination. In determining acceptance for admission, the student's high school academic achievement must count for at least 40 percent by law; this percentage varies according to the individual admission guidelines for each university and college.

Non-Formal Education

Non-formal education in Korea is divided into two types. One is a continuing educational program for youths and adults who have not had the full benefit of a formal education. The other is designed to provide

Vocational training centers have sprung up across the country.

short-term technical or refresher courses to those who are already employed or those in the non-student population.

In the early stages, non-formal education programs placed emphasis on literacy campaigns, education for older children, agricultural extension courses and adult education. It became more diverse in recent years as remarkable changes have occurred in all aspects of Korean life owing to the successful implementation of economic development plans. Skill training programs have now emerged as the main thrust of non-formal education.

Major institutions for non-formal education include civic and trade schools. Civic schools and higher civic schools offer curriculums of one to three years corresponding to regular primary and middle schools for those who desire to advance or to resume regular education at middle or high schools. Trade schools and higher trade schools provide one- to three-year job-oriented programs to those who have finished the regular primary or middle school or their equivalent.

The Air and Correspondence University provides

Vocational training for the handicapped.

working youths and adults with four-year post-high school courses in home economics, business administration, agriculture, pedagogy and public administration. Thirty-minute lectures are broadcast over the radio every day, and those who complete the required credit units receive the same type of degree as the graduates of regular colleges and universities. There are also air and correspondence high school programs.

Non-formal education outside institutions includes various training courses offered by government agencies and private organizations. Their subjects range from special vocational skills to techniques in the arts aiming to assist youths and adults in their job performance or leisure-time activities. In rural areas, youth classes and women's classes are organized as part of community education programs. These classes are most often conducted in school buildings or village halls in the evenings.

Special Education

The Education Laws provide that one or more special schools for handicapped children be established in each province and special city. The number offering primary and secondary education has increased steadily during recent years, though public awareness of their importance is still inadequate.

As of 1996, there were 109 institutions for special education across Korea with a total enrollment of 21,860. They include 12 for the blind, 20 for the deaf, 14 for the physically handicapped, 60 for the mentally retarded and 3 for the emotionally handicapped. In addition to general education, these schools offer skills development in order to prepare the physically handicapped for productive jobs. The Ministry of Education sponsors job placement programs and an annual skills competition.

Educational Reform Drive

To successfully prepare for the 21st century, an educational reform plan was unveiled in May of 1995 calling for the creation of an open and lifelong educaton system available to all, highlighted by a fundamental restructuring of the hell-like college admissions examination. President Kim Young Sam pledged to raise education spending to 5 percent of the GNP to promote creativity and self-realization by allowing students more flexibility in their choice of schools and subject, making substantive facility improvements, giving schools more autonomy, and readjusting the grading and admissions systems so that students will be evaluated on their overall abilities rather than a single test score. It is hoped that through these reforms, the Korean education system will be able to produce creative and well-rounded individuals capable of powering Korea through the age of information and globalization.

Transportation and Communications

Transportation

Reflecting the fast pace of local economic growth during the past three decades, transportation facilities and equipment and annual passenger and cargo volume have increased tremendously. Passenger volume, for example, grew from 1.6 billion persons in 1966 to 13.7 billion in 1995.

Koreans have long enjoyed travelling, and with a marked improvement in living conditions in recent years there has been a corresponding increase in the number of people taking to the highways. During the summer vacation season and on the eve of traditional holidays, inter-city bus terminals and railroad stations bustle with people heading for their favorite resorts or their homes in the provinces.

Subways

Seoul's subway system is the eighth largest in the world, carrying 4.6 million people each day. The system's 8 lines extend to a total of 219.1km and shoulder about 28 percent of the city's daily transit load. Line 1 (7.8km) opened on August 15, 1974. It runs east to west through the downtown area, and connects with the National Railroad to suburban Suwon, Inch'ŏn and Uijŏng-bu. Line 2 runs 60.2km through 49 stations, in a circular route that connects all major commercial and residential districts on both sides of the Han-gang River. Line 3 and 4 are 35.2km and 31.7km long, respectively. These lines cross each other and together connect most of the major locations in the city. Line 5 (52.1km), opened on November 15, 1995, runs across Seoul from northeast

Seoul and Pusan have their own subway systems, and more subway-lines are being constructed in major cities.

to southwest. Line 6,7 and 8 are under construction.

In Pusan, Korea's second-largest city, subway line 1 runs 32.5km through 34 stations in major downtown and suburban locations. It was completed in 1985.

During normal hours, subway trains run every 5 minutes in Seoul and every 5.5 minutes in Pusan. At rush hours the trains are more frequent.

The Seoul and Pusan system have the most up-to-date facilities, and stations are decorated in a combination of traditional motifs and contemporary designs. In city-center stations there are many gift shops and speciality stores.

Railways

The total length of railways in Korea is about 6,600km. Railways serve the entire country in a well-organized and extensive network.

In 1995, about 790 million people used Korea's rail transportation. On the rails are some 1,900 passenger cars and 14,000 freight cars, which operate 2,400 times a day nationwide. This includes the super-express train

The Saemaŭl-ho, the super express train.

Saemaŭl, which runs between Seoul and the port city of Pusan several times each day, covering the distance in about four hours.

For traffic safety and efficiency, the Korean National Railroad (KNR) utilizes a Centralized Traffic Control System (CTC) which regulates six lines around Seoul, as well as 838km and 144 railway stations along the Kyŏngbu, T'aebaek and Chung-ang lines. A microwave communication system was installed on the Kyŏngbu (Seoul-Pusan) line in 1977.

In terms of railroad freight, anthracite coal and cement are the two largest items of cargo, followed by petroleum products, ore and fertilizer.

The KNR is subject to become a public corporation. Its new structure will meet more effectively the increasing demand, for efficient transport as Korea continues to develop into an advanced industrial national with highly sophisticated information networks and a well-developed social welfare system.

The groundbreaking ceremony for the construction of a Seoul-Pusan high-speed railway was held on June

30, 1992. The high-speed railway, is to run from Seoul to Pusan in one hour and 40 minutes, and bring most areas of the country within a half day's travel distance. This will greatly contribute to balanced regional development, easing the current serious traffic congestion and conserving energy, thus helping to make Korea a much better place in which to live and work in the 21st century.

Expressways

Expressways connect Seoul with provincial cities and towns, putting any place in mainland Korea within a one-day round trip of the capital.

The Seoul-Inch'ŏn expressway (29.5km) was completed in 1968 to become the first modern highway built in Korea. The completion in 1970 of the 428km Seoul-Pusan expressway marked a great stride forward in the nation's efforts to expand and modernize its transportation network. The expressway passes through such industrial and urban centers as Suwŏn, Ch'ŏnan, Taejŏn, Kumi, Taegu and Kyŏngju. More highways which will contribute to the development of other provincial cities are being constructed.

In 1981, the two-lane Pusan-Masan Highway was expanded to four lanes and dubbed the '88 Olympic Expressway. In 1995, the total length of the nation's highways had reached some 1,825km.

Automobiles

Over 8.5 million automobiles—cars (70.9 percent), buses (7.2), trucks (21.5) and other vehicles—are on the nation's roadways. There are 6,000 transportation firms in Korea, including about 425 city bus companies, 10 express bus companies and 1,800 taxi fleets.

In Seoul, airport shuttles and city buses are all conveniently located and available throughout the city. There are three types of taxis in operation, each with a different fare rate: regular taxis, medium-sized taxis, and

The Riverside Highway runs east-west through Seoul along the Han-gang river.

deluxe taxis. Express buses transport passengers to and from all principal cities and resorts in the country. The 10 express bus companies operating at present have a combined fleet of about 2,600 buses.

International Air Transportation

Korea is close to many of Asia's major cities, and flight connections can easily be made to all parts of the world.

Seoul's importance in international air traffic grew considerably as a result of the city's successful hosting of the 1988 Olympic Games. Major international airlines conduct over 763 scheduled direct or non-stop flights per week between Seoul and major cities in North America, South America, Europe, North Africa, the Middle East and Asia. Korea has air service agreements with 63 countries: 21 in the Asia-Pacific region, nine in the Middle East, eight in Africa, 19 in Europe and six in North and South America.

In 1969, when the Government turned over management of Korean Air (KAL) to private hands, KAL had only two jet aircraft. Today its fleet of passenger and cargo planes exceeds 100 and continues to grow. During the past decade, the airline registered an average 12 per-

The New Seoul Metropolitan Airport, planned to be capable of handling 100 million passengers annually, will be a hub of Northeast Asia in the early 21st century.

cent annual growth in passenger transportation volume. Korean Air and Asiana Airlines (AAR) now serve 65 cities in various parts of the world, and in 1995 KAL and AAR carried more than 14 million passengers on their international flights.

During the past few years, the Government has made large investments in the improvement of airport facilities to better handle Korea's rapidly growing international air traffic. A new international air terminal was dedicated at Kimpo Airport in Seoul in 1980. The terminal can accommodate 4.8 million passengers and 320,000 tons of cargo annually. As part of Olympics preparations, a new 4,000m runway was built to handle the upsurge in flights. At present, Kimpo Airport, one of three international airports in Korea, is capable of handling 11 million passengers and 1,080,000 tons of cargo annually.

Kimhae Airport near Pusan and Cheju Airport on Cheju-do Island are Korea's other international airports. Like Kimpo, these facilities are equipped with the most modern air traffic control and support systems available. On scenic Cheju, a 3,000m runway able to accommodate jumbo aircraft was completed in 1982. Improvements at the airport are part of a government effort to develop the island as an international tourism destination.

In addition to these facilities, a new Seoul Metropolitan Airport on Yŏngjong-do Island near Inch'ŏn, about 50km west of Seoul, is currently under construction to accommodate Korea's ever-rising international air passenger volume.

Domestic Air

The domestic air routes of both Korean Air and Asiana Airlines serve fourteen cities : Seoul, Pusan , Cheju, Taegu, Sokch'o, Kwangju, Sach'ŏn, Yŏsu, Ulsan, Mokp'o, Kunsan, Kangnŭng, Yech'ŏn, and P'ohang. In 1994, the two carriers transported more than 18 million people on routes within Korea.

Marine Transportation

Korean container ships ply the sea lanes to ports in North and South America, Europe, Australia, the Middle East and Africa. At the same time foreign ocean liners, cruise ships and passenger-carrying freighters pay frequent visits to Korean ports.

The Korea Maritime and Port Administration (KMPA) was established by the Government in 1976 to promote development of the marine transportation industry. As a result of integrated Government and private efforts, by 1994, Korea's fleet had expanded to nearly 10 million gross tons.

In 1995, Korea's total marine cargo volume is expected to reach 470 million M/T annually. Intense competition among the world's carriers to facilitate the transportation of the rising cargo volume will prompt both the shipping and shipbuilding industries to achieve even bigger growth. The annual cargo handling capabilities of Korea's ports are due for expansion as well.

Telecommunications

The 30km telegraph line from Seoul to the west coast city of Inch'ŏn, completed on September 28, 1885, was the first modern communications service in Korea. This service gradually replaced signal fires, which had been the main means of quick communication over long distances. The first telephones in Korea were installed in the royal palace compound in 1896, telephone service was introduced in 1902 and international telephone service was begun in 1924 between Seoul and Fengtian, China. A sufficient modern communications infrastructure, however, was not envisioned until 1962 when a Five-Year Telecommunications Plan was made a part of the First Five-Year Economic and Development Plan (1961-1966). Up until the 1980s, though, the importance of communications to modern society was not fully appreciated. As a result, as late as the end of 1979, there were only 240,000 telephone subscribers or 6.3 telephones per 100 people. Moreover, toll calls and international calls were mostly made through operator assistance, causing great inconvenience and business inefficiency.

In 1982, the Government set up the Korea Telecommunications Authority to take over the telephone and telegraph business from the Ministry of Communications, which is responsible for postal and communications policy. As a result of active R&D investments, Korea, in 1986, became the 10th nation in the world to develop an electronic switching system, called TDX-1, now being used abroad. With this development, Korea has provided an addition one million circuits annually. The number of telephone lines exceeded 10 million in 1987, allowing virtually every household to have a telephone. Also since that year, International Subscriber Dialing (ISD) services have been available to all telephone subscribers. As of the end of 1996, the number of telephone lines reached 22 million and subscribers totaled 19.5

million. The number of telephones per 100 persons had thus increased to 42.2 and all telephone circuits are now connected by automatic switching systems. By the year 2001, a total of 28.23 million telephone lines will have been installed, bringing the telephone supply rate to 51 per 100 persons—on a par with the most advanced nations.

DACOM (DATA Communications Corporation) was also established in 1982 to help bring the nation into the information age. DACOM provides such services as electronic mail, information databases, videotex and value added networks (VAN). It also provides a second international telephone service. From 1988, DACOM has provided a Packet Exchange System, a state-of-the-art telecommunications network which allows the exchange of data through its computer network with 54 countries. DACOM also has a domestic packet network connecting major cities within Korea. Domestic database services are produced and made available by this pioneer service and by the Korea Institute of Industry and Technology Information (KINITI), the Korea Securities Computer Corporation (KOSCOM) for stock information, and other private and government organizations.

In 1984, the Korea Mobile Telecommunications Corporation was established and began both car phone and beeper services. As of 1995, there were 9,657,200 beeper service subscribers. KMT predicts that within the next decade, more sophisticated personal communications networks, or PCNs, will be developed, allowing each person to have a telephone with a private identification number, reachable anywhere in the world at any time.

International transmissions are largely dependent on three satellite earth stations and a microwave communication system and a submarine co-axial cable system between Korea and Japan. They will be reinforced in the future by an additional satellite earth station and global fiber optic communications.

In line with the massive expansion of telecommunication facilities, a plan to construct a state-of-the-art integrated services digital network (ISDN) is being pursued to upgrade the communication network and expedite the creation of an information society. For this various data communication services are being developed and at the same time, the digitalization of terminal equipment as well as transmission media, increasing application of fiber optics and the transition to fully digitalized switching equipment is being undertaken.

Postal Service

Korea's postal service has played a significant role in modernizing the country for the past 100 years since its inception in 1884. Keeping pace with the economic growth of the country, the postal system has grown remarkably into what it is today.

Korea joined the Universal Postal Union in 1900, and is now prepared to take an ever more active part in its work along with other members.

As of 1995, there were 3,450 post offices operating throughout the country, meaning at least every *myŏn* (a group of several villages) was being served by one or more post office.

In 1995, postal mail volume amounted to about 3,455 million items and most letters were delivered by the following working day even though delivery to remote villages might require two to three working days. The volume of mail is constantly growing with an average rate of increase of about 10 percent per year.

The efficiency of mail operations has greatly increased since the introduction of the five digit postal code in July 1970, and the standardization of envelope sizes in January 1974. The revision of the former postal code into six digits was effected in February 1988, to make it more adaptable to the mechanization of mail operations.

Mechanization of mail operations is being expanded and optical character reading machines are being installed at the Seoul Mail Center as a part of the policy to increase the efficiency of mail operations. More machines for mechanization of mail operations will be installed at major post offices in large cities in the future.

To meet the special needs of customers, International Express Mail Service which can provide next day delivery service to specific cities of major countries and the Intelpost (Bureaufax) Service are also being provided. Presently the EMS has networks with 99 countries.

Postal Savings and Insurance Services

All post offices across the nation offer postal savings, postal life insurance, postal money orders, and postal giro services. The postal saving and insurance business started again in 1983.

The number of postal savings accounts was over the 14.6 million as of the end of 1996, and the number of insurance policy holders totaled more than 1.7 million. To provide the public with the convenient services, the ministry has introduced an on-line computer banking network linking 2,700 post offices throughout the country. Almost all the on-line banking terminal machines are manufactured locally. A new on-line postal savings service called the Integrated Passbook System began operation in October 1985.

The Media

Newspapers and Periodicals

As of the end of 1995, there were 114 daily newspapers and 5,998 weekly and monthly publications in Korea. Other periodicals, including bi-monthlies and quarterlies, together with over 1,442 non-commercial periodicals, bring the total number of Korea's newspaper and periodical publications to about 8,448.

The Korean press is now well into its ninth decade. *Tongnip Shinmun* (The Independent), Korea's first modern newspaper, was established in 1896 by Dr. Sŏ Chae-p'il (Philip Jaisohn), a Korean medical doctor and independence campaign leader educated in the United States. This bilingual paper printed 300 copies of four tabloid pages three times a week, the first three pages in *Han-gŭl*, the phonetic Korean alphabet, and the last page in English.

The editorial of the first issue of the *Tongnip Shinmun* read in part: "We propose to become a spokesman for the entire Korean people. We will inform the people about what the government does, and communicate to the government about how the people fare." This sounds rather matter-of-fact today, but almost a century ago in Korea still under the authoritarian rule of a dynasty it was a brave declaration setting the tone for other newspapers which emerged during the most tumultuous transitional period in modern Korean history.

Over the following decades, Korean newspapers found their greatest challenge in upholding nationalistic causes of the Korean people and opening their eyes to the fast-changing world of the 20th century. The newspapers played a significant part in the independence campaigns

More and more newspapers and magazines are hitting the newsstand.

under colonial rule (1910-45) in the face of harsh suppression by the Japanese. After the establishment of an independent government in 1948, the struggle of the print media against injustice and corruption continued.

The *Chosun Ilbo* and the *Dong-A Ilbo* are the two oldest newspapers in Korea, both inaugurated in 1920 in the wake of the famous March First Independence Movement which caused the Japanese colonial government to moderate somewhat its colonial policy. Both newspapers are reputed for their independent and conservative editorial policies and for their influence on public opinion.

Newspaper circulation has been increasing steadily, but it remains the practice of most newspaper companies not to publicize the number of copies they print. The size of circulation is often a zealously guarded business secret.

The Korea Audit Bureau of Circulation (KABC) was established formally on May 31, 1989, to audit and confirm the standardized statements on circulation and distribution data reported by newspapers, magazines and other periodicals which carry commercial advertisements. Korea's ABC reports are to be made public sometime in the near future.

In Korea, subscriptions and advertising account for 30 and 70 percent, respectively, of total newspaper revenues. In 1995, the total revenue from newspaper advertisements amounted to 2.1 trillion *won* (US$2.9 billion), or 43.3 percent of the total revenue from advertising.

Korean newspapers have made significant investments in press facilities and equipment in recent years. Major dailies, for example have built new, modern buildings and realized extensive innovations in the publishing process. Most national dailies operate computerized typesetting and editing systems and have multicolor printing capability.

As a consequence of political reforms and on-going democratization, Korea's press today is no longer the staid and rigid institution it has been in the past, but rather is a free-wheeling and dynamic force which, with broad leeway to criticize officialdom, has become instrumental in promoting social change, modernization and development.

News Agencies

Shortly after liberation in 1945, Korea's first news agency, the Haebang T'ongshin or Liberation Press, was established. This was followed by the emergence of several news agencies over the following decades. Most, however, were shortlived due to a lack of professional expertise and poor finances.

In 1980, two leading general news services, Hapdong and Orient Press, were combined to form Yonhap News Agency. Yonhap, a cooperative of all Korean news media and the first of its kind in the country. It is now the sole general news agency operating in Korea.

Yonhap has expanded its domestic and foreign news coverage extensively since the merger. For nationwide domestic news coverage, it maintains a staff of over 288 reporters and writers in its head office in Seoul and 114 correspondents throughout the country. It maintains 13 overseas bureaus in Europe, North America, the Middle East, Southeast Asia, and South America.

Yonhap has contracts and news exchange agreements with more than 45 foreign news agencies including such major international news services as AP and AFP. Aside from providing foreign and domestic news dispatches in Korean to its over 500 domestic clients, Yonhap transmits an English news service running 8,000 words daily to 130 overseas subscribers through a relay system of communication satellites.

Radio

Historical Sketch

Radio broadcasting in Korea started in 1927 when the Japanese established a station in Seoul after two years of experimental broadcasting. This station operated solely as a mouthpiece for Japan's colonial policy until liberation in 1945.

The U.S. military government in Korea took it over in September 1945 and formed the Korea Broadcasting System (KBS). This was the only radio station in the country until 1954, when a privately-owned and operated network, the Christian Broadcasting System (CBS), started educational and religious programs along with news and entertainment broadcasts.

In December 1956, another Christian station, the Evangelical Alliance Mission, inaugurated the Far East Broadcasting Station in Inch'ŏn, transmitting programs in Korean, English, Chinese and Russian for 100 hours a week. The first commercial radio in Korea, the Pusan Munwha Broadcasting Station, was set up in Pusan in April 1959. The establishment of a number of private broadcasting companies followed, including the Munwha Broadcasting Company (MBC), the Dong-A Broadcasting Station (DBS) and the Tongyang Broadcasting Company (TBC), all located in Seoul.

MBC began operations in December 1961 with the call sign KLKV and has contributed greatly to the development of commercial radio service in Korea. MBC was followed by two rivals, DBS in 1963 and TBC in 1964. DBS, affiliated with Dong-A Ilbo, covered only Seoul and its vicinity. MBC and TBC, affiliated with the Joong-ang Ilbo, had countrywide networks with satellite stations in major provincial cities.

In 1966, the Seoul FM Broadcasting Company put into operation a station, marking the beginning of FM broadcasting in Korea. Three other FM stations were set up in 1970, the Korea Munwha FM station in Seoul, the Pusan Munwha FM station in Pusan and the Korea FM station in Taegu.

The Asia Broadcasting Co., an affiliate of the U.S.-headquartered, non-profit Far East Broadcasting Co. (FEBC), was set up 1972 on Cheju-do Island off Korea's south coast to transmit messages of freedom, peace and hope to Asia.

Two special broadcasting systems also were established in Korea, the Republic of Korea Army Radio and the American Forces Korean Network (AFKN).

The Korean Station was established in 1954 to broadcast informational, educational and entertainment programs for ROK armed forces personnel. The American facility began operations in October 1950 to provide news, features and entrainment programs for U.S. military personnel and their families based in Korea.

Present State

The media merger action taken in the fall of 1980 brought about the greatest change in the history of Korean radio broadcasting. The public Korean Broadcasting System (KBS), already the largest network with 20 local stations, took over two of Seoul's four major private broadcasting companies—the Dong-A Broadcasting System and the Tongyang Broadcasting Company-plus three privately-run provincial radio stations. The Christian Broadcasting System, together with its four provincial stations, was directed to specialize in purely evangelical programs. KBS also took over a 65-percent interest in the Munwha Broadcasting Company with 19 affiliated provincial stations, but MBC was allowed to continue as a privately-run company.

There are also two special stations—the Kukdong Broadcasting System and the Asia Broadcasting System—which air special programs designed mainly to carry out Christian evangelism directed to North Korea, the former Soviet Union, the People's Republic of China and Mongolia as well as South Korea.

KBS has maintained an overseas broadcasting network since 1953. With the introduction of two programs in Indonesian and Arabic in 1975, and two programs in German and Portuguese in 1983, the network has broadcasting services in 11 languages. The others are Korean, English, French, Chinese, Spanish, Russian and Japanese. Programs are beamed to neighboring countries in the Far East, to North America, Hawaii, Europe, Southeast Asia, the Middle East and South America.

The American Forces Korean Network (AFKN) provides AM and FM radio and television service for U.S. military personnel and their dependents in Korea. Its programs, on the air 24 hours a day, are in English and include a news report every hour.

Another wave of change began to break over Korean broadcasting in 1990. Structural reform was engendered by reaching a solution to a number of problems associated with the existing publicly-operated broadcasting system. One reform measure was the emergence of privately-operated broadcasting stations to complement government-operated stations.

Another development was the establishment of a number of specialized broadcasting stations. The Seoul city operated TBS (Traffic Broadcasting Station) was inaugurated in June 1990, followed in December by the government-operated EBS (Educational Broadcasting Station). The privately-owned Seoul Radio Station began broadcasting in March 1991, with a target audio region including Seoul and the surrounding areas of Kyŏnggi-do Province that comprise the greater Seoul Metropolitan area.

There are a total of 103 radio stations in Korea, including 49 FM stations as of June 1996. The most popular radio hour is 12 noon to 1 p.m., and popular programs are news, foreign pop music, serial dramas, classical music, variety shows and sports, in that order.

Despite the spread of television in Korea, radio still has an expanding audience. However, the role and function of radio have undergone necessary changes in recent years, due mainly to the influence and popularity of television. One of the important tasks radio must undertake in the years ahead is not to compete with TV, but to search out its own program areas such as news, music and traffic situation reports and develop them to meet the needs of average listeners.

Television

Historical Sketch

Television broadcasting began in Korea in 1956 with the opening of a privately-owned and commercially-operated station in Seoul. That first TV station was destroyed by fire in 1959.

On December 31, 1961, the official KBS-TV was inaugurated by the government in Seoul as the first full-scale television service in Korea. A commercial operation, TBC-TV, began broadcasts in December 1964 as a sister station of the Tongyang Broadcasting Company, covering Seoul and its immediate vicinity. In the same year, TBC-TV opened a subsidiary station in Pusan to reach the southern part of the country. The Munwha Broadcasting Company established Korea's third television station, MBC-TV, in August 1969. It later was expanded to a countrywide network of 19 local stations. As privately-owned stations came on line after 1990 as a result of structural reform, SBS-TV, a private firm, began broadcasting to the greater Seoul Metropolitan area in December 1991. In May 1995, other local private TV firms also started broadcasting to the Pusan, Taegu, Kwangju, and Taejon areas.

Present State

There are 46 television stations in Korea, and all TV broadcasting is in color. There also is AFKN-TV, operated by the U.S. military in Korea for its personnel and their dependents. It, too, broadcasts in color.

On weekdays, Korean TV stations operate 10 1/2 hours, from 6 a.m. to 10 a.m., and from 5:30 p.m. to midnight. On weekends, broadcasts are extended to 18 hours, from 6 a.m. to midnight.

When KBS-TV started operations in 1961, there were only about 25,000 television sets in Korea. The number of registered sets exceeded the one million mark in 1973 and reached 2,809,000 by the end of 1976. The number jumped to 5,133,000 by the end of 1978, and exceeded seven million by the end of 1982.

As of February 1995, the total number of color television sets registered with KBS exceeded 14.3 million, an average of more than one set for each and every household in Korea. In addition, there are several million black-and-white television sets still in use throughout the country.

Peak time for television viewing is from 8 p.m. to 10 p.m. Favorite types of programs include serial dramas, foreign movies, comedy and quiz shows, sports and news, in that order. Students, however, prefer music shows, sports, movies, comedies, quizzes, specials and serial dramas.

Television has become an important mass medium due to its obvious audiovisual appeal and influence. The initial primary function of television has been entertainment, but recently it has placed more emphasis on information and education, making it a more serious competitor for radio stations and newspapers.

Though television has achieved marked success both in quality and quantity, there still are many areas for improvement. Programming is one area that needs immediate attention, and improvement of educational television is another. Television also must be prepared technically for further advances in the age of satellite TV communications. The mass production of transistorized television sets at low cost is another task that requires prompt attention.

In 1984, Korea television networks introduced the "Olympics in the Home" program by covering almost all the Los Angeles Olympic Games competition around the clock. The success of that undertaking gave Korean broadcasting circles added confidence for the giant task of handling the 1988 Summer Olympics in Seoul. KBS was in charge of Olympic TV operations as host broadcaster for the Seoul Games, setting up an elaborate center at its headquarters to meet successfully the needs and demands of domestic and foreign broadcasters.

Cable TV

Cable TV was first introduced into Korea in 1970. Small-scale commercial interests began to relay live programs, taped serial dramas, and videos to viewers with poor TV reception due to blocking geographical features or manmade structures. By the end of the 1980s, though, the increasing public demand for information and the concurrent advances in telecommunications technology made wide-access cable TV both a necessity and a possibility.

Consequently, the government decided in December 1991 to allow the introduction of full-fledged cable TV.

With the implementation of cable TV broadcasting, Koreans now have another new information source for the 21st century.

Cable firms are classified into three categories; 1) network operators, who supply the cables and converters which connect subscribers to the 2) system operators, which transmit the channels and programs of the 3) program providers. Program providers are subject to the authority of the Minister of Information, while network operators fall under the Minister of Information-Communication.

In 1993, a total 20 TV program providers were designated by the government in 11 program categories including news, sports, dramas and movies, as well as two network operators. In 1994, the government selected 53 system operators, who started broadcasting on March 1, 1995. As of 1996, 29 CATV channels in 15 program categories including 3 public channels are in operation.

Culture and the Arts

Korean art possesses several distinguishing characteristics that create a unique style of its own. Korean art respects nature, and the extensive use of quiet and subdued colors is manifested in Korean paintings and ceramics.

Humor is another characteristic of Korean art. Bold exaggeration, the acceptance of non-symmetrical cubic objects, and unique spatial beauty conveyed by imperfect roundness are examples of humor in Korean art.

Quiet harmony may be cited as another characteristic of Korean art. This means that there is no excess, the right materials being selected in scale with the surroundings.

With all of these characteristics, the Korean arts have inherited a unique aesthetic sense which depicts beauty with honesty and simplicity that is free of artifice.

World Cultural Heritage List

For the first time, three of Korea's most prized national treasures were included on the World Cultural Heritage List of UNESCO on December 9, 1995, joining 469 other cultural and natural monuments in 105 countries. The Korean national treasures so honored are the eighth century Pulguksa Temple and the affiliated artificial stone grotto of Sŏkkuram in Kyŏngju in Kyŏngsangbuk-do Province and the 13th century *Tripitaka Koreana preserved at Haeinsa Temple in Kyŏngsangnam-do* Province, both in the southeastern part of the nation and Chongmyo, the Chosŏn (1392-1910) Royal Ancestral Shrine, located in the capital city of Seoul.

Korea joined the Convention Concerning the Protection of the World Cultural and Natural Heritage in 1988. It is intended to protect outstanding monuments, buildings and sites from man-made destruction and damage. Inclusion on the list identifies the sites as part of the cultural heritage of all humanity. It is a matter of national pride for Korea to have the excellence of its national treasures recognized by the international community through inclusion on the World Heritage List.

Literature

Korean literature shows a significant difference between before and after Western influences. In the pre-Western period, literature was influenced by Shamanism, Buddhism and Confucianism. Under these influences, individuals accepted the status quo and were held accountable for their fatalistic viewpoint. Early literature depicted a love of nature and man and held that nature and man are one.

Another special aspect of the early period of Korean literature was that it began as an oral tradition. Therefore, many literary works are also tales and legends sung or spoken by ancestors of various Korean tribes and were presented at tribal rites, religious festivals, sacrifices and political gatherings.

Influenced by social norms, mores and customs, in Korean literature good is rewarded and evil is punished. Early literature stresses behavior patterns like loyalty to the king, filial piety, respect for seniors, true friendship and chastity for women.

After Western influences, modern Korean literature has shown dissent, both political and moral, and has deviated from traditionally-restricted subject matters to encompass varied themes.

The first Korean writing was produced in the Shilla Kingdom in the 8th century. The script-type language partially adapted from Chinese letters by phonetic sounding was called *Idu*. Only 25 poems called *Hyangga* remain in this style.

During the Koryŏ Dynasty, a popular type of verse called "Longer Verses" came into fashion. At the latter part of the dynasty, a new kind of lyric, *sijo*, gained popularity. The *sijo* usually consisted of three-line stanzas conveying compact messages. After the *Han-gŭl* alphabet was invented, various kinds of love-poetry were attempted.

In the mid-Chosŏn Period, the lyrical form known as *kasa* was widely composed. Written in Chinese as a kind of typical Korean lyric verse, the literati expressed their attachment to the beauties of nature through their *kasa*.

After the introduction of *Sirhak* (Practical Learning) in the 17th and 18th centuries, Western influence brought new developments to Korean literature, often through Christianity. The concept that all men are equal became a common theme and attacked the inequality of traditional society.

One great change in the literature field was the outpouring of works in *Han-gŭl*. Authorship also diversified from the literati to commoners.

New Stories of the Golden Turtle written in Chinese by Kim Si-sŭp (1435-1493) is usually regarded as the beginning of fiction in Korea. Only the first book, containing five stories, survives today. The stories are marked by Korean settings and tragic endings in contrast with the Chinese settings and romantic happy endings that characterized earlier works.

Hŏ Kyun's *Hong Kiltong* is considered the first vernacular-novel. Written in the 17th century, it is a social commentary that attacks the inequalities of Chosŏn society.

In the 19th century, *p'ansori*, or the "one man opera" form gained popularity. *P'ansori* were tales sung by professional artists to an outdoor audience. The text of *p'ansori* usually contained satirical messages that lampooned the upper class.

In the years before and after annexation by Japan in 1910, the new national consciousness depicted through the medium of literature was written in *Han-gŭl*, called *shinmumhak*, or new literature.

Ch'oe Nam-sŏn published the inspiring poem, "From the Sea to a Child," in the magazine *Sonyŏn* (Child) in 1908, giving birth to modern poetry or free verse in Korea. Also, Yi Kwang-soo started to write modern novels in the magazine *Ch'ŏngch'un* (Youth) in 1914, and his contribution to modern Korean literature is highly regarded.

Up to the late 1960s, creative talents expressed themselves in this genre. Favorite themes were social injustice, the dehumanizing influence of industrialization and modernization.

Recently, works of noted writers such as Yi Mun-yŏl and Han Mu-sook have been translated into various foreign languages including English and French. Since the quality of writing and translation continues to rise, in the near future it is hoped that the works of Korean writers will be appreciated in other countries as much as they are in Korea.

Painting

Korean painting represents a pattern of cultural achievement typical of the creative vigor and aesthetic sense of the Korean people.

Korean painting has developed steadily throughout its long history from the Three Kingdoms period (57 B.C. — A.D. 668) to modern times. The earliest examples of the Three Kingdoms' paintings are found on the walls of Koguryŏ tombs in southern Manchuria and near P'yŏngyang (third-fourth century); and in Tomb 155 in Kyŏngju, capital of Shilla (sixth century).

It is said that while the paintings of Koguryŏ are dynamic and rhythmic and the paintings of Shilla are somewhat speculative and meticulous.

In the Koryŏ Period (918-1392), painting flourished in great variety, inheriting the artistic tradition of Unified Shilla which marked the golden age of painting. Ar-

Mt. Inwangsan after Rainfall by Chŏng Sŏn (1676-1759).

tists of the era created temple murals and Buddhist scroll paintings, marking a flourishing Korean Buddhism. Many master painters produced works of the so-called "Four Gentlemen" (the plum, orchid, chrysanthemum and bamboo) portraits and Buddhist paintings.

During the early Chosŏn Dynasty (1392-1910), distinguished painters were still unable to free themselves from conservatism, remaining engrossed in the official style of the Chinese Northern and Southern Schools.

A significant departure took place during 18th century Chosŏn. Chŏng Sŏn (1676-1759) was awakened to the national identity of Korean painting, and subsequently poured his passion into painting the real landscape of Korea. Among his works, "Mt. Inwangsan after Rainfall", "The Diamond Mountain" and "Fresh Breeze Valley" show his characteristic uniqueness .

In the latter half of the 18th century, European science and technology were introduced to Korea by Catholic missionaries, and the *Sirhak* (Practical Learning) movement led artists to seek the truth in reality. They began

Mask Dance by Kim Hong-do (1745-?).

to paint secular paintings on the themes of daily life of the common people called genre paintings. This trend can be said to reflect Chosŏn Dynasty's changing attitude toward modern society.

As the pioneering artists in genre paintings, Kim Hong-do (1745-?) and Sin Yun-bok (1758-?) left several notable works which give us a taste of what life was like in Chosŏn society.

Paintings by anonymous artists, though less sophisticated in style than those by the Confucian artist-scholars, dealt more with the daily life of average Koreans and their aspirations and dreams. Colorful and vivid, these paintings were free of conventional restraints. They attract remarkable interest today both in and outside of Korea.

Following the political disorder and Japanese annexation of Korea in 1910, the traditional styles of painting tended to deteriorate under Japanese colonial policies. Western oil painting was introduced at this time and

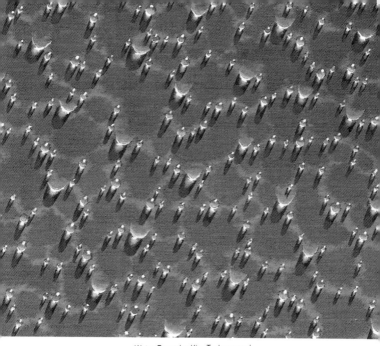

Water Drops by Kim Tschang-yeul.

grew to be very prevalent.

After liberation from Japanese rule in 1945, the tradition of Korean painting was revived by a number of outstanding artists. A great number of Korean artists educated in Europe and the United States have played a major role in introducing to Korea up-to-date trends and styles in contemporary art. Both traditional Oriental painting and Western-style oil painting flourish in present-day Korea with several prominent artists displaying creative genius and originality.

Sculpture

The oldest known examples of sculpture in Korea are some rock carvings on a riverside cliff named Pan-gudae in Kyŏngsangbuk-do Province and some clay, bone and stone figurines of men and animals excavated from Neolithic village sites. Similar figurines were actively produced in bronze, earthenware and clay during the Bronze Age. However, it was not until the introduction

Sŏkkuram Grotto in Kyŏngju is one of the oldest and most beautiful Buddhist sculptural monuments in the world, dating back to the 8th century.

of Buddhism to the Three Kingdoms in the fourth century that sculpture began to develop significantly in both quality and quantity. Each of the Three Kingdoms, Koguryŏ, Paekche and Shilla, was enthusiastic supporters of the newly introduced religion, and consequently the carving of Buddhist images and pagodas became the main thrust of their artisans. With artistic and religious fervor, they carved numerous Buddhist images as well as pagodas of diverse shapes in bronze, stone and wood. The regional differences of the Three Kingdoms were gradually integrated along with the assimilation of T'ang Chinese arts. Buddhist sculpture enjoyed a "golden age" during the two centuries following Shilla's unification of the Peninsula in 676. The Sŏkkuram Grotto shrine, built in the mid-eighth century near Kyŏngju, represents the best Buddhist sculpture of this period.

As the Koryŏ Dynasty proclaimed Buddhism as its state religion, Buddhist carvings continued to flourish during the period, which produced a great number of Budd-

To closely get in touch with the masses,
modern sculpture comes to the streets.

hist images and pagodas of excellent artistic quality. Buddhist sculpture rapidly declined with the inception of the Chosŏn Dynasty in the late 14th century, as its ruling aristocracy suppressed the religion as a national policy. Sculptural art in general experienced a notable deterioration during the entire Chosŏn Period because its Confucian-dominated society held it in little esteem.

In spite of a brilliant tradition of stone and bronze sculpture in the ancient and medieval periods, Korea saw the birth of modern sculpture only recently. The first sculptor of significance in modern times was Kim Pok-chin who studied in Japan in the late 1910s. Any growth in this field was frustrated during the colonial period, and most sculptors simply imitated Western techniques. Korean art circles began to gain some vitality after the Korean War (1950-53) and modern sculpture became a world of its own in the 1960s, when the opposing schools of realism and abstractionism grew and sculptors began to use a great variety of materials.

Two gilt-bronze Maitreya, early 7th century.

Metalcraft

A variety of bronze relics, including mirrors, axes, knives and bells, all dating from the Bronze Age, have been discovered all over Korea. These artifacts, decorated with interesting geometric and animal patterns, are evidence of the advanced craftsmanship of ancient Korean metalsmiths.

The art of metalcraft made steady progress through the early Iron Age and by the time the Three Kingdoms of Koguryŏ, Paekche and Shilla emerged in the first century B.C., quite a high level of sophistication had been reached. Archaeologists found that the large mounded tombs of the Shilla (57 B.C.-A.D.935) aristocracy are a great source of brilliant metalcraft objects produced by ancient Korean artisans. The tombs have yielded rich collections of fantastic gold accessories of kings and

The Emille Bell, the largest Korean Bell, dates back to the late 8th century.

queens, such as crowns, earrings, necklaces, bracelets and girdles. The gold crowns in particular attest to a remarkable standard of artistic sophistication. Linear engraving and repoussé work embellish the upright tree-shaped ornaments, the diadems and the pendants, which are further decorated with gold spangles and comma-shaped jade attached with fine wire. The earrings show a refined filigree combined with granulation.

Shilla artisans also excelled in the production of temple bells. The bronze bells of Shilla were renowned for their elegant design, sonorous sound and impressive size. The late 8th-century *Divine Bell of King Sŏngdŏk*, or *Emille Bell* as it is popularly known, is the largest of existing temple bells in Korea. It is decorated with beautiful designs of lotus-shape medallions, flowers, flames and heavenly maidens.

Pottery

Ceramics are by far the most famous Korean art objects among the world's art historians and connoisseurs. From the Neolithic earthen pots with their rustic surfaces to the elegant celadon vases adorned with exquisite inlaid patterns, Korea boasts a great legacy of ceramics.

The early ceramic pots from the Neolithic period have narrow, rounded bases and are decorated with parallel lines and dots or "comb patterns." Some painted pottery and clay figurines evolved later. A vast amount of stoneware recovered from Shilla tombs shows the next stage of development in pottery making. Varying in color from gray to black and sometimes brown tones resulting from the degree of oxidation in the kiln, these early stoneware pieces are free and original in style, some carrying unmistakable evidence of shaman influence.

Shilla stoneware produced after the fifth century, however, tended to be less spirited, possibly due to the influence of Buddhism. Many potters applied stamped designs to duplicate the same patterns on funerary urns used to contain the ashes after cremation. Gradually during the Unified Shilla period(668-935), pottery became sturdier but more unassuming, without the pleasing ingenuity of the earlier periods.

From the 12th to the 13th century during the Koryŏ Dynasty, the art of pottery making in Korea reached its apex with the development of a mysterious bluish-green celadon glaze and the inlaying technique. Celadon techniques originally came to Korea from China during the Sung period (960-1279), possibly from the T'zu-yao kilns in the 10th century. However, Chinese influences were disregarded by the first half of the 12th century, and indigenous creativity achieved its highest degree of refinement.

The technique of inlaying, which was devised by Korean potters, involved incising designs into the clay

Koryŏ celadon with inlaid designs.

and filling the recesses with white or black slip. Excess slip was scraped away prior to firing. These designs, applied in a simple and restrained manner in the early stage, gave a subtle and dignified beauty to celadon vessels.

By the end of the 13th century, however, potters became unrestrained in the use of these popular designs, abandoning the long tradition of molding their wares in various fascinating shapes inspired by familiar motifs in nature. Craftsmanship further deteriorated and inlaid designs became coarse after the Mongol invasion of Korea. During the 14th century, the skills of celadon making finally vanished, and the secret of producing the lustrous range of blue-green glazes would remain lost until rediscovered in the 20th century.

The dominant social influence of the Chosŏn Dynasty was Confucianism and this shift from the leisurely aristocratic Koryŏ Period to the more pragmatic social concepts of Confucianism is reflected in ceramic art. White porcelains were the dominant style of the Chosŏn Period.

During the Chosŏn, the kilns were controlled by the government and produced inlaid white porcelains as well as inlaid blue celadons. The white porcelains in underglaze blue were usually decorated with the pattern of the "Four Gentlemen" (plum blossoms, orchids, chrysanthemums and bamboo) and with the lotus flower, arabesque designs and autumn grass.

From the mid-19th century, Korea's ceramic arts deteriorated in both technique and shape, reflecting the decline of the dynasty itself.

However, Ich'ŏn, in Kyonggi-do Province, only one hour away from Seoul, has survived as a potters haven for almost 600 years, even though many of the present-day craftsmen began working after the Korean War.

The town has remained famous for its pottery because of its high-quality clay and mineral-free water. Minerals can contaminate the clay and result in unwanted colors.

In addition to the kilns, there are numerous pottery shops and museums to display each kiln's products and to provide background on the history of porcelain and ceramic ware.

Most of the Ich'ŏn kilns these days produce traditional pottery, imitations of Koryŏ celadon and Chosŏn porcelain. A few potters produce modern table settings.

Architecture

Pre-modern Korean architecture may be classified into two major styles: those used in palace and temple structures, and those used in the houses of common people, which consisted of many local variations. For the former, Korea's ancient architects adopted the bracket system.

A traditional Korean House.

The latter was characterized by thatched roofs and heated floors called *ondol*. People of the upper classes built larger houses with tiled roofs. The roofs were elegantly curved and accentuated with slightly uplifting eaves.

The natural environment was always regarded as an element of supreme importance in Korean architecture. Numerous Buddhist temples across the country, for instance, were located in mountains noted for their scenic beauty, and their structures were carefully arranged so as to achieve an ideal harmony with the natural surroundings. In selecting the site for a building of any function, Koreans tended to attach special meaning to the natural environment. They did not consider a place good enough for a building unless it commanded an appropriate view of "mountains and water." This pursuit of a constant contact with nature was not only due to aesthetic reasons, but also because geomantic principles dominated the Korean psychology.

Western architecture was first introduced to Korea with the opening of its doors to the world toward the end of the 19th century. Churches and offices for for-

Modern sculpture decorates many building sites in Seoul.

eign legations were built by Western architects and engineers during those years.

In the early years of modern architecture's development, Koreans learned new ideas and skills from Western architects and engineers. Among these early pioneers in the 1930s were Pak Tong-jin who designed the main building of Korea University.

Korean architecture entered a new phase of development during the post-Korean War reconstruction with the return of two ambitious young architects of great talent from overseas—Kim Chung-up from France and Kim Su-keun from Japan. Both architects have greatly contributed to the development of Korean architecture. Some structures of special note in Seoul include Kim Su-keun's Olympic Stadium, Um Tok-mun's Sejong Cultural Center and Kim Seok-chul's Seoul Arts Center.

Seoul has rapidly changed into a fascinating showcase of modern architectural trends and styles. The city's ever-changing skyline speaks for the dramatic speed with which the nation has developed in recent years.

Music

Traditional Korean music can be divided into two kinds—*Chŏngak* and *Minsokak*. The former refers to the entire musical tradition of the upper classes; the latter is folk music or the music of the common people, even when performed for the aristocracy.

The *Chŏngak* tradition includes incidental music originally used in court rites such as sacrifices, royal audiences and banquets.

Whereas *Chŏngak* melodies are usually slow, solemn and complex in their intertwining of long, elaborate melodic lines, folk music incorporates shaman and Buddhist ritual songs, farmers' music, *sanjo* (virtuoso solo music with percussion accompaniment) and *P'ansori* (dramatic story-singing). They are usually colorful, vibrant and appealing to the emotions.

Western music first appeared with the introduction of a Christian hymnal, Ch'ansongga, in 1893. The official inclusion of Western music in the schools occurred for the first time in 1904 and it rapidly permeated into Korean urban and intellectual society.

In 1919 Hong Nan-pa composed *"Pongsŏnhwa,"* a tremendously popular composition which is one of the earliest pieces in Korean music history to be composed in the "Western style." With the appearance of this song, the Korean musical community leaned more and more away from traditional influences.

Following liberation in 1945, colleges and universities in Korea started establishing departments of Western music. Many Korean musicians have studied abroad with outstanding success and returned home to enrich the musical culture of the nation.

A performance of *Chŏng-ak* (Court Music).

Korea's first Western-style orchestra was established in 1945 under the name of Korea Philharmonic Orchestra Society, and there are presently several orchestras in Seoul and other major cities. Opera is also greatly appreciated by Koreans. Many opera groups including the National Opera Group, the Kim Cha-kyong Opera group and the Seoul Opera Group have emerged since Verdi's La Traviata was performed by Korean musicians for the first time in 1948.

Nowadays, an increasing number of Korean musicians are performing in concerts and other fields abroad. Many have won highest acclaim from foreign critics and audiences. A number have taken top awards in international competitions, and some have assumed prestigious

posts as conductors or in other musical roles. Conductors working abroad include Chung Myung-hun who is the former music director and principal conductor of the French National Bastille Opera.

The Korean Traditional Performing Arts Center was established in 1951 and contributes to maintain and develop traditional Korean music.

In 1993, The School of Music in the Korean National Institute of Arts, the first ever Western-style conservatory was founded at the Seoul Arts Center in Sŏcho-dong, southern Seoul. Boasting a high-powered faculty, the conservatory aims to put the nation on the international cultural map.

Today, Korean music can be broken down into three

A Korean Court Dance, *Sŏnyurak* (Boat Dance).

basic categories; (1) Korean native, (2) Western-oriented, (3) an experimental combination which attempts to reconcile East with West.

Dance

Traditional dance in Korea comes in six varieties; shaman, Buddhist, Confucian, court, folk and mask.

Confucian and Buddhist influences are very important. It has been said that the Confucian influence has been mainly repressive, while Buddhism's more lenient attitude has contributed to developing beautiful court dances and many shaman rituals for the dead.

Dancers from the ancient periods mainly tried to express a deep ecstatic power. They were not interested in acrobatic physical motions, but in expressing metaphysical joy.

A large number of traditional dances withered away during the nation's 36-year-long colonial rule by Japan and rapid industrialization and urbanization of Korea

Chinju *Kŏmmu* (Sword Dance).

in the past three decades. It was in the 1980s that people started focusing their attention to reviving the long-forgotten dances.

Of the 56 original royal court dances, only the *Kŏmmu* (Sword dance) of the Shilla period (57 B.C.-A.D. 935), the *Hakmu* (Crane dance) of the Koryŏ period (918-1392), the *Kiakmu* (Instrument music dance) of the Paekche period (18 B.C.-A.D. 660) and *Chunaengmu* (the nightingale-singing-in-the- spring dance) of the Chosŏn Dynasty (1392-1910) are still famous.

All of these dances have been designated as "intangible cultural properties" by the government for their perpetuation, and performers have been granted the titles of "Human Cultural Assets," the highest honor awarded to masters of traditional arts and crafts.

The development of early modern dance in Korea was largely thanks to the work of pioneers like Cho T'aekkwon and Choi Sung-hi, who originally studied Korean traditional dance and were later educated overseas as well.

After liberation in 1945, the Seoul Ballet Company was founded in 1950. Im Sung-nam, a leading male dancer, returned home in 1956 after studying ballet in Japan. He established a ballet studio in Seoul and contributed to the national progress of ballet.

Today, Korea boasts approximately 40 traditional Korean dance groups, 30 modern dance companies including modern dance groups led by Yook Wan-soon and Hong Shin-ja and 10 ballet troups including the Universal Ballet Company, a private professional performing group which was organized in 1984.

Drama and Movies

Korean drama has its origin in prehistoric religious rites, and music and dance plays an integral part in all traditional theatrical performances. A good example of this classical theatrical form is the masked dance called *t'alch'um*, a half-pantomime, half-dance featuring earthy satire and humor. Varying slightly from one region to another in style, dialogue and costume, it enjoyed remarkable popularity among rural people until early this century. *P'ansori*, lengthy narrative folk songs relating popular tales, and *kkoktukakshi norŭm*, or puppet plays, performed by vagabond artists also drew large audiences, while the shamanistic rites called *kut* fulfilled an entertainment as well as religious role during the premodern period.

Korea's first Western-style theater, Won-gaksa, was opened in Seoul in 1908. Until that time, entertainers presented their works either on a makeshift stage or in any village square large enough to accommodate an audience. Western-style drama was first staged at this newly opened theater, leading to a period of so-called new school drama of popular romances.

In the 1920s, a more serious movement was initiated by a group of Western literature students in Tokyo who translated and performed modern Western realistic plays. They were more academic than commercial, but

Korea's traditional dramatic masked dances.

the movement had an enduring impact on Korean dramatists of succeeding generations. Drama notably dwindled in the face of the booming motion picture industry in the 1960s and then television. The '70s saw a number of young artists studying and adopting the styles and themes of traditional theatrical works like the masked dance plays, shaman rituals and *p'ansori*. The Korean Culture and Arts Foundation sponsors an annual drama festival to encourage theatrical performances.

The first Korean-made film was shown to the general public in 1919. Entitled *Righteous Revenge*, it was a so-called kino-drama designed to be combined with a stage performance. The first feature film, *Oath Under the Moon*, appeared in 1923. In 1926, the classic *Arirang*, a protest against Japanese oppression, produced by actor-director Na Un-gyu drew an enthusiastic response from the public. Early Korean movies had patriotic and anti-Japanese overtones, which appealed to the Korean public suffering under colonial exploitation. As all cinematic activities were controlled by the Japanese by the end of the 1930s, movies degenerated into chauvinistic propaganda.

The film industry did a booming business for about a decade from the mid-1950s. But the next two decades were largely a time of stagnation due largely to the rapid development of television and decreasing public interest, among other factors. Since the early 1980s, however, the film industry has gained some vitality owing chiefly to a few talented young directors who boldly discarded old stereotypes. Their works have been shown in festivals in Cannes, Chicago, Berlin, Venice, London, Tokyo and Moscow, and have captured a number of awards.

Printing and Publishing

In 1966, a small scroll of printed Buddhist scripture entitled *Pure Light Dharani Sutra* was found inside a stone pagoda at Pulguksa Temple in Kyŏngju. The scroll was discovered to have been published under Shilla patronage around A.D. 751, more than one century earlier than China's *Diamond Sutra* which previously had been considered the world's oldest surviving wood-block print.

During the 13th-century Koryŏ Dynasty, Koreans realized another wondrous achievement in printing history by carrying out the titanic task of carving over 80,000 woodblocks containing a complete rendition of Buddhist scripture. The project was motivated by the desire to enlist the aid of Buddha in thwarting Mongol incursions, particularly as a first edition of the work, compiled two centuries earlier, was destroyed by the northern intruders. Entitled *Tripitaka Koreana*, this second edition is still preserved in excellent condition in ancient archives at Haeinsa Temple.

Historic records show that Koreans first used movable metal type in printing a book on etiquette around 1234, long before Gutenberg brought out his Bible in 1455. The earliest verified example of movable-type printing is a collection of Zen Buddhist sermons, printed in 1377 during the Koryŏ period. A copy of this edi-

One of the largest bookstores in downtown Seoul. Nowadays most of them
are equipped with user-convenient facilities, and are usually packed with youngsters.

tion is currently preserved at the French national library
in Paris.

Korea's thriving publishing business today is built
upon this printing tradition and respect for scholarship.
Despite the rigid qualifications required of publishers,
some 7,381 publishing houses were in operation as of
the end of 1992. Likewise, there has recently been a notable trend toward proliferation of specialized magazines,
ranging from house-keeping, sports and leisure activities to science and technology, health care, literature and
art.

With the exception of student textbooks, 24,783 titles, totaling 136.7 million copies, were published in
1992. Topping the list was literature with 4,654 titles,
followed by juvenile interest books with 4,149. Next
came science and arts with 2,948 titles, followed by social sciences with 2,874, religions with 2,044, arts with
1,130, history with 953, languages with 938, philosophy
with 608, pure science with 328, and general works with
232. School reference books came to 3,925 titles.

The National Folk Museum in Seoul.

Museums and Theaters

Korea abounds with cultural facilities of all levels and categories where people can enjoy exhibitions and stage performances throughout the year. These places offer real glimpses of the cultural and artistic achievements of Koreans past and present, of both traditional and modern trends and tastes. From full-scale museums of international standards to small theaters where performers and spectators can intermingle for face-to-face communication, they vary in type and scale so as to satisfy the diverse interests and penchants of the communities they serve.

There are eight museums financed and operated by the central government. Of these, the National Museum of Korea and the National Folklore Museum are in Seoul, while the other six are located in provincial cities, some of which were the capitals of ancient kingdoms. These cities are storehouses of historic remains and relics that

The National Theater in Seoul.

shed light on the cultural past of their particular region. Therefore, each museum has a unique historical flavor.

In addition to the national and public museums and college and university museums, there are more than a dozen private museums in Korea. These museums were established by private citizens, religious organizations or business enterprises. In most cases, their collections consist of historic materials which took their collectors almost a lifetime to gather. The collections range from folk paintings, books, religious objects, furniture and embroidery to traditional costumes.

Korea has about a dozen multi-purpose theaters. The National Theater, founded in 1950, is located at the foot of Namsan Mountain in the heart of Seoul. Its purpose is to preserve and develop traditional culture and contemporary performing arts. Since its founding, the Theater has grown to maturity and won popular acclaim, reflecting developments in the world of theater in general. Having gone through four decades of hardship and

The Seoul Arts Center-located in southern Seoul.

change, the National Theater is now proud of its seven resident companies, which are the National Drama Company, the National Changgŭk (Korean musical drama) Company, the National Dance Company, the National Ballet Company, the National Chorus Company, the National Opera Company, and the National Traditional Music Orchestra. The seven resident companies of the National Theater currently stage some 35 regular productions annually. In additon, the companies work on many special trip productions to foreign countries and every corner of Korea. Its main hall can seat 1,518 spectators, the small hall can seat 454 spectators, and the Nori-madang (Korean-style open-air theater) can seat 1,200 spectators.

The National Museum of Contemporary Art, located on the grounds of a scenic park south of Seoul, has an

extensive collection of Korean and Western art objects
of the 20th century. The number of art galleries has greatly increased during recent years along with the ever-
growing interest in fine art among the general public.

The largest of multi-purpose theaters is the Sejong Cultural Center in Seoul. Affiliated with this municipal performing arts center, which opened in 1978, are the Seoul
Philharmonic Orchestra, the Seoul City Orchestra for
Traditional Music, the Seoul Municipal Dance Company, the Seoul Municipal Choir and the Seoul Municipal
Junior Choir. The center's main theater can seat 4,000
spectators and its pipe organ is one of the finest in the
world.

One recent major event on the cultural scene was the
completion of the Seoul Arts Center in southern Seoul
on the slope of Mt. Umyŏn. Ten years of construction

The National Museum of Contemporary Art in the suburbs of Seoul.

work was finally finished on the Seoul Opera House which was opened in February 1993. The Opera House is the centerpiece of the art center with a capacity of 2,346.

The center, with a total land space of over 234,385 square meters and a total floor space of 120,951 square meters, has two elegant concert halls, a fine arts gallery, a calligraphy hall, an arts library and a film archive.

The main auditorium of the Concert Hall has seats for 2,600 people. There also is a Recital Hall that can seat 400. The Festival Hall, the largest building planned in the center complex, was designed to house three theaters—an Opera House with 2,346 seats, a Play House with 800 seats and a Studio Theater with 300 seats. Drama, opera, ballet, dance and combinations of those art forms made up the scheduled programs, featuring companies and performers from both Korea and abroad.

Way of Life

Traditional Houses

Traditional Korean houses remained relatively unchanged from the Three Kingdoms period (57 B.C.-A.D. 668) to the late Chosŏn Dynasty (1392-1910). The houses developed various aspects to be suitable for the differing climates of the cold north and the warmer south.

The under-floor heating system, or *ondol* first used in the north channeled smoke and heat through flues under the floor, was used in traditional houses along with wooden floors from the warmer south, producing a unique house seen in no other country in the world.

The major materials of traditional style houses are earth and wood. The earth insulates the inside from outside heat or cold. Black-grooved tiles for the roof are made of earth, usually red clay. Also, the construction of the Korean house did not use nails but was assembled with wooden pegs.

Simple traditional houses with a rectangular floor and a kitchen and a room on either side developed into an L-shaped and then a U-shaped or square shaped house with a courtyard at the center.

Upper class houses consisted of a number of separate structures, one to accommodate women and children, one for the men of the family and their guests, called the "sarangch'ae," and one for servants, all enclosed within a wall. A family ancestral shrine was built behind the house. A lotus pond was sometimes created in front of the house outside the wall.

A family, wearing the Korean traditional costume, *hanbok*, strolls in a traditional Korean house.

Clothing

The Korean traditional costume, *hanbok*, has been handed down in the same forms for men and women for hundreds of years, unchanged because they are well suited to climate and culture.

The man's basic outfit consists of a *chŏgori* (jacket), *paji* (trousers) and *turumagi* (overcoat). The jacket has loose sleeves, and the trousers are roomy and tied with straps around the ankles. The women's *hanbok* includes a *chŏgori* (short jacket) with two long ribbons, which are tied to form the *otkorŭm*, and has long full sleeves and a full length, high waisted wrap around skirt called the *chi'ma*. White cotton socks and boat-shaped shoes, made of silk, straw or rubber, are worn with these costumes.

The beauty of Korean dresses can be founded in the simple design and harmony of lines and colors of upper and lower pieces.

A Korean full-course dinner consists of a variety of vegetable and mountain herb dishes, grilled fish, roast beef, and *shinsŏllo,* a type of stew cooked in a brass chafing dish.

Food

Rice, either plain or cooked with other grains, is the main dish at Korean meals. Rice is accompanied by a variety of side dishes that vary greatly according to the region and the season. Next to rice comes *kimch'i,* a spicy vegetable dish generally comprised of celery, cabbage and turnips or cucumbers seasoned with salt, garlic, onions, ginger, red pepper and shellfish. Soup is also a vital part of almost every meal. Other dishes include seafood, meat or poultry, greens, herbs and roots.

Each person has his own rice and soup bowls but all other dishes are placed in the center of the table for everyone to partake of. A spoon and chopsticks are used for eating.

A favorite dish is *pulgogi,* strips of beef roasted over a brazier at the table after being marinated in a mixture of soy sauce, sesame oil, sesame seeds, garlic, green onions and other seasonings. Koreans generally like hot, spicy foods, so red pepper is an indispensable seasoning.

Family Life

In traditional Korea, the typical family was large with several generations usually living together. Many children were desired for stability and security and there were often a dozen or more family members. With modernization, however, such large families are disappearing. Newly married couples these days tend to live on their own, instead of living with other family members.

In a Korean home, the head of the family was traditionally regarded as the source of authority. The head of the family issued strict instructions and others obeyed them without question. Obedience to the superior was considered natural and a most admirable virtue. It was understood that the patriarch of the family would be fair in dealing with all family members.

Koreans have traditionally believed that a man must first cultivate himself and manage his family properly before he can govern the nation. Men have traditionally been given the responsibility of representing, supporting and protecting the family, as well as the power to command. Order at home is maintained through obedience to superiors, that is, children obeying parents, the wife the husband, the servants the master, and so on. This Confucian decorum has dominated Korean life and way of thinking over the centuries and is still respected in all forms of human relations.

Koreans still place great emphasis on filial piety to parents and ancestors, fidelity to spouse and faithfulness to friends, although loyalty to the ruler and respect for teachers appear to have more or less lost their reigning importance among the five most esteemed ethical values in traditional society. Korean fables and legends abound with episodes of filial sons and daughters as well as faithful wives who even risked their lives to prove their loyalty to family.

Korean family life is changing rapidly with moderni-

Bowing to one's parents and elders is an age-old New Year's custom.

zation and equalizing rights between men and women. The revised Family Law which went into effect in January 1991 has accelerated equality. The law establishes equal property rights for men and women and gives a choice to divorcing women for the first time in regard to property rights and custody of any children.

An increasing number of young couples live independently, adapting to changing ethic values and social environment.

Names

Korean names almost invariably consist of three Chinese characters that are pronounced with three Korean syllables. The family name comes first and the remaining two characters form the given name, of which one character often identifies the generation.

There are about 300 family names in Korea, but only a handful of them cover the vast majority of the population. Among the most common names are Kim, Yi, Pak, An, Chang, Cho, Ch'oe, Chŏng, Han , Kang, Yu and Yun. Korean women do not change their name with marri-

On *Hanshik* day, falling in early April, and *Ch'usŏk,* in the fall, many Korean families visit the ancestral tombs to pay their respect.

age. Koreans do not refer to others by their given name except among very close friends. Even among siblings, the younger ones are not supposed to address the elder ones by given names.

Festivals and Holidays

The pageantry, merrymaking and colorful rites of holiday festivals are an important feature of Korean life. However, with the powerful tide of Westernization and modernization since the turn of the century, most traditional holidays are just remembered rather than observed. But there still are some important festive days on the Korean calendar that are celebrated joyfully and elaborately.

The first day of the first lunar month, which is called *Sŏl* by Koreans and usually falls in late January or early February, has traditionally been the biggest holiday. The entire family gathers together and, dressed in their best clothes, observes ancestral rites. After the ceremonies, they enjoy a feast and the younger members of the fa-

Kanggangsuwŏllae, a traditional circle dance, is performed under the full moon to celebrate *Ch'usŏk*, the harvest moon festival.

mily make a deep, traditional bow to their elders. Although the New Year generally continues to be celebrated by the lunar calendar the solar New Year is also observed with two days of official holiday.

Other major holidays include *Taeborŭm*, the first full moon of the year, when farmers and fishermen pray for rich corps and enjoy special games; *Tano*, the fifth day of the fifth lunar month, when farmers take a day off from the field for joint entertainment; *Ch'usŏk*, the 15th day of the eighth lunar month, a harvest festival and day of thanksgiving; and Buddha's Birthday, the eighth day of the fourth lunar month, when believers observe special services at temples and stage colorful lantern processions.

There are several family holidays that are important to all Koreans and celebrated with much feasting. They are *paegil*, the hundredth day after a child's birth; *tol*, the first birthday; *hwan-gap*, the 60th birthday, which is considered especially important for this is the day when one has completed the 60-year cycle of the Oriental zodiac; and *kohi*, the 70th birthday.

In addition to the traditional holidays based on the lunar calendar, Koreans observe the following designated national holidays.

National Holidays

January 1: *New Year's Day*—The first two days of the New Year are generally celebrated.

First Day of the First Month by the Lunar Calendar: *Sŏl*—This day, which is also known as Lunar New Year's Day, is observed with family rituals honoring ancestors, special food and traditional games.

March 1: *Independence Movement Day*—Koreans observe the anniversary of the March 1, 1919 Independence Movement against Japanese rule.

April 5: *Arbor Day*—On this day, government officials, teachers, school children and thousands of Koreans throughout the country plant trees in accordance with the government's reforestation program.

May 5: *Children's Day*—This day is celebrated with various programs for children, who enjoy themselves to the full with their parents.

Eighth Day of the Fourth Month by the Lunar Calendar: *Buddha's Birthday*—Solemn rituals are held at Buddhist temples, and the day's festivities are climaxed by a lantern parade.

June 6: *Memorial Day*—On this day the nation pays tribute to its war dead. Memorial services are held at the National Cemetery in Seoul.

July 17: *Constitution Day*—This day commemorates the adoption of the Republic of Korea Constitution in 1948.

August 15: *Liberation Day*—On this day in 1945, Korea was liberated from Japan after 35 years of colonial rule. The day also marks the 1948 establishment of the government of the Republic of Korea.

Fifteenth Day of the Eighth Month by the Lunar Calendar: *Ch'usŏk or Harvest Festival Day*—This is one of the great national holidays of the year. On this day a feast is prepared and families hold memorial services at the family grave site. Viewing the full moon is a feature of the evening.

October 3: *National Foundation Day*—This day marks the traditional founding of Korea by Tan-gun in 2333 B.C.

December 25: *Christmas Day*—Christians and other citizens celebrate this holy day as in the West.

Religions

Freedom of religion is guaranteed by the Constitution, and many of the world's major religions are active in the Republic of Korea. Korea's most ancient religions are Shamanism, Buddhism and Confucianism. All these played an important role in the country's early cultural development and have greatly influenced thought and behavior. Christianity was introduced approximately 200 years ago, but has spread rapidly to claim one of the largest followings. There are also various minor religions syncretizing elements of these traditional religions.

According to 1995 social statistics survey, 51.1 percent of Koreans follow a specific religious faith. Buddhists number 10,388,000 or 45.6 percent of the religious population; Protestants 8,819,000 or 38.7 percent; Catholics 2,988,000 or 13.1 percent; and Confucianists 193,000 or 0.8 percent.

Status of Religion
(As of 1995)

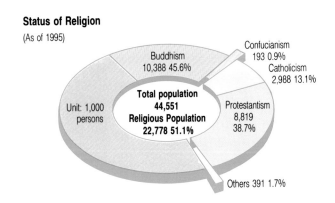

Confucianism 193 0.9%
Buddhism 10,388 45.6%
Catholicism 2,988 13.1%
Unit: 1,000 persons
Total population 44,551
Religious Population 22,778 51.1%
Protestantism 8,819 38.7%
Others 391 1.7%

Shamanism

Spirit worship or nature worship is Korea's oldest belief, the origin of which is lost in primeval mystery. It is based on the belief that human beings are not the only possessors of spirits, but that they also reside in natural forces and animate or inanimate objects.

The shaman, or *mudang* in Korean, is an intermediary with the spiritual world and is considered capable of averting bad luck, curing sickness and assuring a propitious passage from this world to the next. Korean shamanism includes the worship of thousands of spirits and demons that are believed to dwell in every object in the natural world, including rocks, trees, mountains and streams as well as celestial bodies. One of the important aspects of Korean shamanism is its deep belief in the soul of the dead. The shaman is expected to resolve conflicts and tensions that are believed to exist between the living and dead.

This system of belief persists in Korea today. A shaman today is almost invariably a woman, unlike in the past when the intermediary could be either male or female. Shamanism for the traditional Korean is a religion of fear and superstition, but for the modern generation, it is a colorful and artistic ingredient of culture. A shaman ceremony, rich with exorcist elements, combines theatrical elements with music and dance.

The introduction of more sophisticated religions like Taoism, Confucianism and Buddhism did not result in the abandonment of shamanistic beliefs and practices. They assimilated elements of shamanistic faith and coexisted peacefully. Shamanism has remained an underlying religion of the Korean people as well as a vital aspect of their culture.

Buddhism

Buddhism is a highly disciplined philosophic religion which stresses personal salvation through the renunciation of worldly desires, thus avoiding rebirth in the endless cycle of reincarnations, and bringing about the absorption of the soul of the enlightened into Nirvana.

As this religion spread from the place of its origin in India, however, all sorts of local superstitions and theological systems were absorbed into it, producing an elaborate array of deities, saviors, bodhisattvas, heavens and hells that the historic Buddha never mentioned. It was this type of Buddhism, called Mahayana or the Greater Vehicle, that reached Korea in the fourth century, brought by missionary monks from India and China.

Under royal patronage, this new faith spread with remarkable force through the Koguryŏ and Paekche Kingdoms. Many temples and monasteries were constructed and hordes of believers converted. By the sixth century monks and artisans were migrating to Japan with scriptures and religious artifacts to form the basis of early Buddhist culture there.

By the time Shilla unified the peninsula in A.D. 668, it had embraced Buddhism as the state religion, though it managed its government systems along Confucian lines. Royal patronage during this brief golden age of Unified Shilla produced a magnificent flowering of Buddhist arts and temple architecture. The rapid decline of the kingdom in less than two centuries did not harm Buddhism, as the rulers of the succeeding Koryŏ dynasty were even more enthusiastic in their support of the religion.

During Koryŏ, many monks became politicians and courtiers. A number of them were corrupt and contributed to the kingdom's decline. Buddhist arts and architecture continued to flourish with lavish support from aristocratic households.

When General Yi Sŏng-gye staged a revolt and had himself proclaimed king in 1392, he removed all influence of Buddhism from the government and adopted Confucian teachings as the guiding principles for state management and moral decorum. Throughout the five-century reign of the Yi Dynasty, or Chosŏn, all efforts at Buddhist revival were met with strong opposition from

Celebrating Buddha's birthday.

Confucian scholars and officials. Official oppression continued until the last years of Chosŏn.

When the Japanese took over as colonial rulers in 1910, they made attempts to assimilate Korean Buddhist sects with those of Japan. These attempts by and large failed and even resulted in a revival of interest in native Buddhism among Koreans. Under Japanese influence, some Korean monks discarded the long tradition of clerical celibacy, and after liberation in 1945 there were bitter legal battles for many years over the legitimacy of ownership of temple estates between the married and celibate sects.

Buddhism in Korea is undergoing a sort of renaissance and making efforts to adapt to the changes of modern industrial society. Buddhist orders have set up urban

A ritual in celebration of Confucius' birthday.

centers for the propagation of the faith, coming out of their long seclusion in the mountainside temples and hermitages.

Confucianism

The thought of Confucius embraced no consideration of the supernatural, except for an impersonal divine order referred to as heaven, which left human affairs alone as long as relative order and good government prevailed on earth. In this sense, Confucianism was a religion without a god, like early Buddhism. But as ages passed, the sage and his principal disciples were canonized by later followers as a means of inculcating their doctrines among simple and uneducated people.

Confucian literature entered the peninsula along with the earliest specimens of written Chinese material around the beginning of the Christian era. The three kingdoms of Koguryŏ, Paekche and Shilla all left records that indicate the early existence of Confucian influence. In Koguryŏ for example there was a central Confucian university functioning by the fourth century A.D., and in the provinces there were private Confucian academies. Paekche established similar institutions at about the same time. Shilla, as usual, was the last to embrace foreign influence.

The court of Unified Shilla sent delegations of scholars to T'ang China to observe the workings of Confucian institutions firsthand, and to bring back voluminous writings on the subject. Buddhism was the state religion, but Confucianism formed the philosophical and structural backbone of the state. Even with the establishment of the Koryŏ Dynasty in the 10th century, the form of government did not materially change, except that the influence of Buddhism became more pronounced.

The Confucian-oriented Yi Dynasty, or Chosŏn, often criticized for political power struggles and clan feuds deriving from differing interpretations of Confucian doctrine, actually achieved a golden age of renaissance.

Confucianism in Korea was manifested a system of education, ceremony and civil administration. The civil service examination, or *kwagŏ*, adopted after the Chinese system in the late 10th century, greatly encouraged studies in the Confucian classics and deeply implanted Confucian values in Korean minds. Even today, Koreans can hardly be said to have discarded the customs, habits and thought patterns derived from Confucian teachings.

Christianity

The tide of Christian mission activity reached Korea in the 17th century, when copies of Catholic missionary Matteo Ricci's works in Chinese were brought back from Beijing by the annual tributary mission to the Chinese emperor. Along with religious doctrine, these books included aspects of Western learning such as a more accurate calendar system and other matters that attracted the attention of scholars of *Sirhak*, or the School of Practical Learning.

By the 18th century, there were several converts or

The head of the Korean Catholic Church, delivering a sermon.

potential converts among these scholars and their families, but no priests entered Korea until 1785, when a Jesuit, Father Peter Grammont, crossed the border secretly and began baptizing believers and ordaining clergy. The number of converts continued to increase, although the propagation of foreign religion on Korean soil was still technically against the law and there were sporadic persecutions. By the year 1863, 12 Korean priests presided over a community of some 23,000 believers.

With the coming to power in 1863 of Taewŏngun, a xenophobic prince regent, persecution began in earnest and continued until 1876, when the prince regent lost power and Korea was forced to sign treaties with Western powers. In 1925, 79 Koreans who had been martyred during the Chosŏn Dynasty persecutions were beatified at St. Peter's Basilica in Rome, and in 1968 an additional 24 were beatified.

Dedicating a newly-enlarged Christian church.

During and following the Korean War (1950-53), the number of Catholic relief organizations and missionaries increased. The Korean Catholic church grew quickly and its hierarchy was established in 1962. The Roman Catholic Church in Korea celebrated its bicentennial with a visit to Seoul by Pope John Paul II and the canonization of 93 Korean and 10 French missionary martyrs in 1984. This was the first time a canonization ceremony was ever held outside the Vatican. It gave Korea the fourth largest number of Catholic saints in the world.

Protestant missionaries of all persuasions began to stream into Korea after the opening of its ports. The first was Horace N. Allen, an American medical doctor. The missionaries came as bearers of modern knowledge in every field, filling a vacuum which the isolated, indrawn Korean nation desperately needed to fill if it was to attain the much desired modernization and maintain independence. The missionaries arranged for many of

Korea's young potential leaders to go abroad for advanced education and assisted their patriotic resistance to Japan.

After annexation in 1910, many foreign missionaries gave direct and indirect support to the Korean independence movement in the face of severe persecutions by the Japanese. These efforts continued until their expulsion in 1940 on the eve of World War II. Since the Korean War, the Protestant churches have experienced such phenomenal growth that today there are 113 denominations in Korea in 1995. The Presbyterians and Methodists have the largest memberships.

Ch'ŏndogyo

There are more than 240 so-called new religions in Korea. Most of these modern movements, varying in membership from as many as 600,000 to a mere handful, are characterized by syncretism, each espousing

The main cathedral of Ch'ŏndogyo

veneration of a different divine leader or savior sent down from heaven to redeem the world. Most of these beliefs are Confucian in ethics, have Buddhist-type rites, and follow Taoist methods in religious practice.

The most noteworthy of these movements, and apparently providing a sort of doctrinal framework for the others, is *Ch'ŏndogyo*, or the Religion of the Heavenly Way. This outspokenly nationalist religion was initiated as a social and theological movement against rampant corruption and foreign encroachments in the 1860s. At that time it was called Tonghak, or Eastern Learning, in contrast to the "Western learning" represented by Catholicism. The movement developed into a peasant revolution in the early 1890s and later changed its name to *Ch'ondogyo*. Leaders of this religion took important roles in anti-Japanese campaigns during the colonial period.

Islam

The first Koreans to be introduced to Islam in modern times were those who moved to Manchuria in the early 20th century under Japan's colonial policy. A handful of converts returned home after World War II, but they had no place to worship until Turkish troops came with the United Nations Forces during the Korean War and allowed them to join their services. The inaugural service of Korean Islam was held in September 1955, followed by the election of the first Korean Imam (chaplain). The Korean Islamic Society was expanded and reorganized as the Korean Muslim Federation in 1967, and a central mosque was dedicated in Seoul in 1976. There are about 20,000 Muslims in Korea today.

Sports and Leisure

The opening ceremony of the
'88 Seoul Summer Olympics.

The development of sports has been particularly emphasized in recent years as a government policy to promote physical fitness and to enhance national prestige by improved performance at international competitions. Aided by rapidly rising income levels, the last several years have seen the construction of all kinds of sports facilities and increased endeavors to carry out an efficient athletic policy. As a result, sports have become a part of everyday life, and spectator sports in particular are becoming increasingly popular.

The Ministry of Sports was established in 1982 to promote physical education and sports throughout the country and provide the necessary government assistance for the successful staging of the 1986 Asian Games and the 1988 Summer Olympics. In 1993, the ministry was merged with the Ministry of Culture to form the Ministry of Culture and Sports. The Seoul Olympic Sports Promotion Foundation, established in 1989, is responsible for raising and administering funds for national sports promotion and for elevating the level of athletics. The Korea Sports Council (KSC) governs all amateur sports activities. The association is comprised of 45 individual sports federations.

The Seoul Olympics in Retrospect

The Games of the 24th Olympiad were successfully concluded after a 16-day run in Seoul from September 17 to October 2, 1988, under the motto "Peace, Harmony, Progress." They turned out to be the largest Olympiad ever up to that point with more than 13,000 athletes and officials from 160 countries gathering to promote

the lofty ideal of harmony and peace by transcending barriers separating East and West and North and South. The first boycott-free Olympics in 12 years, they went beyond ideological divisions and national interests to put the Olympic movement back on track.

The success of the Seoul Games was the result of the all-out efforts Koreans made to achieve harmony and peace for the entire human race, the undaunted spirit of the International Olympic Committee to revive the Olympics as a genuine festival of mankind, and the aspiration for peace shared by nations around the globe. Domestically it was also due to the 26,000 volunteer workers of all age groups, the families who opened their

The Olympic Park.

homes to some 500 of the Olympic visitors, the citizens who willingly participated in a traffic-control system based on even-odd license plate numbers (which was 95 percent successful), and some 3,180,000 spectators who enthusiastically cheered the athletes from around the world.

Facilities

Partly as a result of the 1988 Seoul Olympics, Korea has many world-class sports facilities. They are concentrated in Seoul and Pusan where most of the Olympic events were held.

The Seoul Sports Complex, completed in 1984, encompasses a land area of 545,000 square meters. Located just south of the Han-gang River, it includes the Olympic Stadium with a seating capacity of 100,000, two gymnasiums for basketball and boxing, an indoor swimming pool, a baseball park and a warmup field. It is 14 kilometers, less than half an hour drive, from downtown and 30 kilometers, about 45 minutes, from the airport. It can be reached by subway.

The Olympic Park, occupying a vast area of 1,500,000 square meters in southeastern Seoul, comprises a 6,000-capacity velodrome, three gymnasiums with a combined capacity of 26,000 for gymnastics, fencing and weightlifting events, an indoor swimming pool that can accommodate 10,000 spectators, and 18 tennis courts with seating for 15,000 including a 10,000-seat center court. It is about 5 kilometers east of the Seoul Sports Complex, 18 kilometers from downtown Seoul and 35 kilometers from the airport.

Also constructed for the Olympics was an equestrian park in the suburbs of Seoul, a regatta course on the Han-gang River and a yachting marina in Pusan, the large port city on the southern tip of the Peninsula.

A key training facility for the country's sports competitors is the T'aenŭng Athletes Village located in the eastern outskirts of Seoul.

Built on a 7.2-hectare (17.1 acre) site in the midst of a beautifully wooded area, the village includes a skating rink, an indoor swimming pool, a shooting range and gymnasiums for wrestling, boxing and weightlifting. The training camp also has six dormitories that can accommodate 578 athletes, billets for foreign coaches, strength-measurement equipment and a medical facility with a dispensary, where advanced athletic training techniques are studied.

A second training center, a branch of the T'aenŭng Athletes Village, was opened in 1984 in the southern port city of Chinhae. It was designated to facilitate training during the winter season.

Marathoner Sohn Kee-jung, gold medalist in the Berlin Olympics in 1936, and Hwang Young-cho, gold medalist in the Barcelona Olympics in 1992.

International Competitions

Korea is an active participant in many international competitions and has emerged as a rising power in a number of sports including soccer, basketball, archery, table tennis, hockey, handball, wrestling and boxing. Korea participated in the London Olympics in 1948 for the first time under its own flag. In 1936, a Korean marathon runner, Sohn Kee-jung, won a gold medal in Berlin, but he ran as a member of the Japanese team because Korea was under Japan's colonial rule at the time.

Korean athletes have been constantly improving their Olympic performances. They won one gold, one silver and four bronze medals in the 1976 Montreal Games to rank 19th among more than 100 participating nations. In Los Angeles in 1984, Koreans captured six gold, six silver and seven bronze medals, ranking 10th in a field of 140 nations, in the 1988 Seoul Olympics, they won 12 gold, 10 silver and 11 bronze medals to rank fourth in a field of 160 nations. In the Asian Games, which is the largest sports festival in the region, Korea ranked third in New Delhi in 1982 after the People's Republic of China and Japan, and second in Seoul in the 1986 Asian Games, trailing China by one gold. Korea also fared well at the 1990 Games Beijing and the 1994 Hiroshima Games, garnering 54 and 63 gold medals, respectively. It is thus fitting that the 2002 Asian Games will be held in Pusan.

In the 1992 Barcelona Summer Olympic Games, Korea placed seventh in the final medal standings with a total of 29 medals, with 12 gold, 5 silver and 12 bronze. Its performance surpassed all the other Asian nations except China. The Korean team's athletic skill was evidenced by first-place finishes in a broad array of sports events including archery, badminton, weightlifting, sharpshooting, wrestling, handball, judo, and the marathon. Hwang Young-cho's gold in the marathon enabled him to become the nation's first distance runner to win the race under the Korean national flag. The Korean team set a new Olympic record in men's rifle shooting. In the weightlifting competition, Chun Byung-kwan set an Olympic record on his way to winning the bantamweight division.

The nation has played host to many international sporting events, not to mention the '88 Seoul Olympics. Since the 42nd World Shooting Championships, the first ever in Asia, were held at the T'aenŭng International Shooting Range in Seoul in 1978, many world and Asian championships and international competitions have been hosted by Korea.

Since 1971, Korea has annually sponsored an international football tournament, originally known as the President's Cup Football Tournament and now renamed as the Korea Cup, which has greatly contributed to the improvement of soccer skills in Asia and to understand-

Korea will cohost the World Cup finals in 2002 with Japan,
the first such event to be held in Asia

ing and friendship among the participants. The tournament has drawn teams from Asia, Europe, Latin America and Africa. Korea, along with Iraq, represented the Asian region in the World Cup Soccer Tournament held in Mexico in 1986, in which the world's 24 strongest teams participated. During the 1990 World Cup in Rome, Korea participated along with the United Arab Emirates as representatives of the Asian region and in the 1994 U.S. World Cup with Saudi Arabia. The three consecutive selections serve as testimony to the fact that Korean players have earned their ranking among the world's best. This impressive record, as well as Korea's popular enthusiasm for soccer, led to the decision of the FIFA executive committee in Zurich on May 31, 1996 that Korea should cohost the World Cup finals in 2002 with Japan, the first such event to be held in Asia.

National Events

The National Sports Festival is held every October for competition in 27 different sports by participants from all over the nation. The festival is held on a rotation basis in all major cities, including Seoul, Pusan, Taegu, Kwangju and Inch'ŏn, generating a string of festivities and serving as a springboard for the nation's dynamic development of athletic competitiveness. The Children's National Sports Festival is also held annually for primary and middle school students, drawing over 7,000 boys and girls from across the country. The National Winter Sports Festival, held every January, includes speed skating, figure skating, skiing, ice hockey and the biathlon.

Another annual event is the National Sports Festival for the Handicapped. Held each year since 1981, it brings together people from all over the country and provides the opportunity for them to demonstrate their special skills. The 13th festival in May 1993 drew 1,700 participants.

Traditional Sports

Among several categories of traditional sports that have been revived in modern times, the martial art of *T'aekwŏndo* is the best known internationally. This self-defense martial art has become a popular international sport in the last quarter century. Some 1,500 Korean instructors are teaching it in more than 100 countries.

In Korea, the *T'aekwŏndo* Association has a membership of about 3,500,000, constituting the largest affiliate of the Korea Sports Council. The World T'aekwŏndo Federation (WTF), with its headquarters in Seoul, was officially approved as the controlling body of the sport by the International Olympic Committee in 1980. T'aekwŏndo was a demonstration sport in the 1988 Seoul Olympics. It will be an official Olympic medal event beginning in the 2000 Summer Olympics to be held in Sydney.

Ssirŭm is a form of wrestling that has been popular

Taekwondo has become a popular international sport(top);
Ssirŭm, traditional Korean wrestling, has gone professional(bottom).

in Korea since the Three Kingdoms period (57 B.C.-A.D. 668). This Korean-style wrestling with simple rules was widely performed in all village festivals, the winner receiving a big bull in most contests. The Korean Ssirŭm Association has succeeded in generating a nation-wide boom in this traditional sport by sponsoring spectacular matches. *Ssirŭm* has become firmly established as one of the most popular spectator sports in the nation.

Leisure

The leisure industry is one of the fastest-growing industries in Korea as an increasing number of people engage in various leisure activities as a result of high economic growth and the rising living standard in recent years. Koreans, by nature, are outgoing and throw themselves into play with as much intensity as they work.

The many museums, palaces, temples, royal tombs, parks and scenic and historic sites scattered all across

Para-gliding and other leisure sports have become popular as Koreans have more free time.

Korea have always been popular sites for family outings and picnics. In recent years, many people seem to find physical exercise another good way to spend their free time while promoting physical fitness. Tennis and jogging are the two most popular morning sports among town-dwellers. Those who are more athletically-oriented organize morning soccer teams with neighbors. Among other sports pursued by enthusiastic hobbyists are swimming, mountaineering, golfing, skiing, water skiing, salt and fresh water fishing, wind surfing and handball. Spectator sports like soccer, baseball, basketball, volleyball, boxing and *ssirŭm* have an avid following.

Recently more and more urbanites have tended to spend their holidays away from home. With the fast increase in privately-owned automobiles in recent years, more families motor out of the city to scenic spots in mountains and beaches on weekends and during holidays. At the same time, watching television and playing *changgi* or *go* remain popular ways of spending weekends among many male office workers.

Tourism

With its scenic beauty and unique cultural and historic heritage, Korea has much to offer tourists. A peninsular country with four seasons, it boasts picturesque beaches, mountains and rivers. There are many ancient Buddhist temples, royal palaces, sculptural images, pagodas, archaeological sites, fortresses, folk villages and museums.

The tourist industry has been growing by leaps and bounds over the last two decades. The number of foreign visitors increased from 84,216 in 1967 to 3,580,024 in 1994. The development of Korea's tourist industry is a natural consequence of its phenomenal economic growth, but the specific allocation of resources has also been a vital factor. The Government enacted a series of tourism promotion laws which resulted in a growth rate of 11 percent annually in tourist arrivals during the last decade. There have been massive projects to explore and develop tourist resources and facilities such as hotel accommodations; land, sea and air transportation; tourist services; national parks; museums; golf courses; and casinos. Most of the tourism development and promotion projects have been spearheaded by the Korea National Tourism Corporation.

The nation's tourist market has been shifting from America to the Asian region over the last two decades. In 1970, Americans accounted for 32 percent of all tourists, with Japanese forming the second largest group. By 1994, however, visitors from Japan comprised 45.9 percent of the total, followed by visitors from North and South America, mainly the United States, at 10.7 percent.

Government regulations are constantly being reviewed and revised to offer greater convenience to visitors. A

Korea has many scenic mountains. Seventy percent of the land is mountainous.

tourist visa is good for three months, and many necessities and souvenir items of both domestic and foreign origin are available tax free. Increasing numbers of tourist guides, proficient in English, Japanese and other languages, are being trained and employed.

Tourists may visit Korea for 15 days without a visa, but proof of confirmed onward air reservations is required. Nationals of some countries do not need visas and may stay up to 3 months in some cases, 2 or 1 month for others provided they do not undertake remunerative activities in Korea.

How to Get to Korea

Airlines: Korea is connected with just about every major capital in the world, either through direct flights or by connecting flights at major international airports in the East Asia. There are about 600 flights in and out of Korea every week.

Korean Air has opened new routes between Seoul and destinations in Europe, America and the Middle East. The flight from Tokyo to Seoul takes about two hours. Both Korean Air, Asiana Airlines and Japan Airlines connect many major cities in Japan with Pusan, Seoul and Chejudo Island. From Hong Kong, passengers can fly direct to Seoul via Cathay Pacific Airways, Asiana Airlines, British Airways, Thai Airways International and Korean Air.

Since 1963, Seoul has been included in the round-the-world air schedule approved by the International Air Transport Association (IATA). This permits any passenger on a round-the-world ticket to visit at no additional charge.

Korean Air and Asiana Airlines provide domestic air transport service, connecting Seoul with Pusan, Taegu, Kwangju, Sokch'o, Kangnŭng, Yŏsu, Chinju, Ulsan, P'ohang, Yech'ŏn, Kunsan, Mokp'o and Chejudo Island. They also connect Chejudo Island with major cities in Korea.

Namdaemun, the South Gate of Seoul (National Treasure No.1), is surrounded by skyscrapers.

Steamship Lines: Various steamship lines provide passenger service to Korea. Among those from the American west coast are Waterman Steamship, American Pioneer, Pacific Far East, Pacific Orient Express, States Marine and United States Lines. A ferry service links Pusan with Chejudo Island and the Japanese ports of Shimonoseki, Kobe and Hakada. Another ferry plies between Inch'on and the Chinese ports of Tianjin and Weihai.

Railway Services: The Korean National Railroad runs three kinds of express trains: super, special and regular. Super express trains link Seoul with Pusan, Mokp'o, Kyŏngju, Kwangju and Yŏsu. The super and special express trains have dining cars, and Pullman cars are connected to all-night express trains. Local trains, which

A picturesque view of Mt.Sŏraksan with clouds.

make frequent stops, are also available.

Guided Tour Services: Guided tours around Seoul, other scenic places and historic sites are offered regularly by many tourist services. A variety of tours are available, including morning, afternoon and night tours, as well as nationwide tours of a week or more duration.

Currency: Korea's monetary unit is the *won*, which is easily exchanged for U.S. dollars, Hong Kong dollars, Japanese yen and British sterling as well as other foreign currencies at banks and major tourist hotels. The basic rate of conversion, subject to change by fluctuations in the market, was about 780 *won* for one US dollar in 1995. Korea's currency comes in 1,000, 5,000 and 10,000 *won* bills, and in 1, 5, 10, 50, 100 and 500 *won* coins.

Ch'angdŏkkung Palace in Seoul. Behind the palace is the elegant and serene Piwon, or "Secret Garden", formerly a private park for the royal family.

Places to Visit

Seoul: Seoul is the world's 10th largest city, where past and present coexist in a fascinating manner. Centuries-old palaces, gates, shrines and priceless art objects at museums attest to the illustrious past of the city, while the glistening facades of soaring skyscrapers and the bustling traffic bespeak its vibrant present. With a population of more than 10 million, the city is not only the administrative capital of the Republic, but also its political, economic, cultural and educational center.

There are four ancient royal palaces dating to the Chosŏn Dynasty (1392-1910) in Seoul: Kyŏngbokkung, Tŏksugung, Ch'angdŏkkung, and Ch'anggyŏnggung palaces. There also is Chongmyo, the royal ancestral shrine of Chosŏn. Piwŏn, or the Secret Garden, adjacent to Ch'ang-

The hustle and bustle of the district of Myŏng-dong, in downtown Seoul.

dŏkkung palace, is another noted place with beautifully landscaped gardens and classical structures. Other places recommended for foreign visitors include the National Museum, the National Classical Music Institute, the Sejong Cultural Center, the Hoam Art Hall, the Namsan Tower and the Korea House. The newly erected National Museum of Contemporary Art at Kwach'ŏn, a southern satellite town, also deserves a visit.

Another experience the visitor should not pass up is a Korean dinner, either at a modern restaurant or a courtly Korean-style restaurant. Excellent Chinese and Japanese food is also available, as well as French, Italian, Mexican, Pakistani and other cuisines. Seoul also has an active night life, with roof-top nightclubs, cabarets and cafes. English is spoken at many restaurants, bars and shops.

Korean Folk Village: A traditional village, located about 30 minutes south of Seoul, reenacts ancient Korean folk life. The village was erected in 1973 and now includes aspects of almost everything uniquely Korean from days gone by. Homes typical of the various provinces can be identified. In the village square, tightrope walkers, wedding or funeral processions, kite-flying contests, and folk dance troupes are seen regularly. The blacksmith, carpenter, potter and instrument craftsman can be seen at work in their shops.

Kanghwado Island: Situated in the estuary of the Han-gang River north of Inch'ŏn port, this is Korea's fifth largest island, an area rich in history and natural beauty. Major historic monuments here include an altar believed to have been erected by Tan-gun, the legendary founder of the nation, fortresses, walls, a celadon kiln dating to the 13th century Koryŏ period, and Chŏndŭngsa Temple. The driving time from Seoul is approximately one and a half hours.

P'anmunjŏm: A 56-kilometer bus trip north of Seoul, this is the truce village where the Korean Armistice Agreement was signed on July 27, 1953, ending the fierce fighting of the Korean War (1950-1953). It is a joint security area managed by the U.N. Command and North Korean guards. Reservations for visits must be made a few days in advance to secure military clearance.

Kyŏngju: This city was the ancient capital of the Shilla Kingdom for a thousand years. Royal tombs, temple sites with weathered stone pagodas and Buddhist reliefs and fortress ruins are scattered all around the city. The mounded royal tombs have yielded many precious antique objects including gorgeous gold crowns and other accessories. Ancient historic records relate that the city, patterned after the T'ang capital with rows of avenues and streets crossing at right angles, had one million inhabitants, and all the houses within the city walls were roofed with tile.

The two supreme treasures of Kyŏngju are the Pul-

A Variety of sightseeing spots in Kyŏngju, all dating back to the 7th and 8th centuries (clockwise from top, left): A Buddha carved on Shinsŏnam rock on Mt. Namsan; Pulguksa Temple; P'osŏkjŏng, a stone channel where water once flowed, used at royal banquets to float cups of wine; Ch'ŏmsŏngdae observatory; Tabot'ap pagoda at Pulguksa Temple.

Mt.Sŏraksan.

guksa Temple and nearby Sŏkkuram Grotto shrine, both built in the eighth century and representing highly refined Buddhist art widely appreciated throughout the Far East. Other important historic sites include: Tumuli Park, Onŭng (Five Tombs), Ch'ŏmsŏngdae (observatory), General Kim Yu-shin's Tomb, and Mt. Namsan which is dotted with numerous Buddhist images, pagodas and temple remains. The Kyŏngju National Museum houses antique treasures recovered from Kyŏngju and its vicinity.

The Pomun Lake Resort, located 6 kilometers from downtown on the eastern outskirts of the city, is a newly developed integrated tourist area with several first-class hotels and various recreational facilities.

Chejudo Island: Korea's only island province is about one hour by air from Seoul, but it takes the traveler to a land of different climate and nature. Cheju enjoys a

The sun rises over the East Sea.

semitropical climate and its plants and landscape are remarkably different from those of the mainland. The principal mountain is the 1,950-meter-high Mt. Hallasan, an extinct volcano with a large crater at its summit. Lava flows from this volcano, which was last active in 1007, have resulted in many tunnels, pillars and other unusual features of quick-cooling basalt. The island is a popular tourist resort and honeymoon destination.

Mt. Sŏraksan and East Coast Resorts: The northern stretch of Korea's east coast, which can be reached by plane, train or express bus from Seoul, is rugged and mountainous, with breathtaking scenery. Skiing and other winter sports help make the area a year-round resort, but the most popular recreations are swimming in summer and mountain climbing in autumn. The beaches are perhaps the finest in Korea, gently shelving into shallow water and mild currents. Sŏraksan Moun-

The rocky coastline carved by the sea.

tain is part of the Kŭmgangsan Range (Diamond Mountains), which are considered one of the world's most spectacular natural wonders.

Along the Southern Coast: The southern coastal regions of Korea have long been popular with Korean travelers, but only recently, with the completion of the Honam and Namhae expressways, have these picturesque coastal routes become easily accessible. The areas around Chinhae, Ch'ungmu, Chinju, and Namhae are recommended as high-lights of this scenic region.

The southern boundary of the Korean Peninsula is a sunken coastline which has created an irregular pattern of bays and inlets with more than 400 offshore islands. In addition to the expressway and rail service, the use of the hydrofoil between Pusan and Yŏsu is recommended, as it stops at Sŏngp'o, Ch'ungmu, Samch'ŏnp'o, and Namhae. Reservations for transporation and hotels can be made in Seoul through travel agencies.

Shopping

Korea is gaining recognition as a mecca for shoppers, offering a great variety of shopping at reasonable prices. Tourists may purchase tax-free goods at any of the hundreds of shops in large department stores and shopping arcades in Seoul and major cities throughout the country. Popular shopping items include jewelry, furs, silk, antique chests, ceramics, lacquerware, brassware, embroidery, personal computers, video and cassette tapes, sportswear, down coats, eel skin and leather products, ginseng and dolls.

Major department stores located in the heart of Seoul include Shinsegae, Lotte, Midopa, Hyundai and Dong-bang Plaza. A network of underground arcades branch out from Myŏng-dong, Seoul's most crowded shopping and entertainment area. Subway entrances and underpasses also lead to these amazing tunnels of shopping bargains. Of all commercial areas in Seoul, however, It'ae-won, which is located adjacent to a U.S. military compound, bustles with the greatest number of foreigners. Insa-dong, or Mary's Alley, is clustered with many antique and art stores, while East Gate (Tongdaemun) Market is famous for silks.